We Wi

SEEK PEACE and

Pursue It

We Will
SEEK PEACE and
Pursue It

REFLECTIONS AND PRAYERS FOR PEACE AND RECONCILIATION

Neil Paynter (Ed.)

wild goose
publications

www.**ionabooks**.com

First published 2015 by
Wild Goose Publications, Fourth Floor, Savoy House,
140 Sauchiehall Street, Glasgow G2 3DH, UK,
the publishing division of the Iona Community.
Scottish Charity No. SC003794. Limited Company Reg. No. SC096243.

ISBN 978-1-84952-428-5

Cover photograph © David Coleman

Overseas distribution
Australia: Willow Connection Pty Ltd, Unit 4A, 3–9 Kenneth Road, Manly Vale,
NSW 2093
New Zealand: Pleroma, Higginson Street, Otane 4170, Central Hawkes Bay
Canada: Bayard Distribution, 10 Lower Spadina Ave., Suite 400, Toronto,
Ontario M5V 2Z

Printed by Bell & Bain, Thornliebank, Glasgow

They will beat their swords into ploughshares
and their spears into pruning hooks.

Nation will not take up sword against nation,
nor will they train for war any more.

The wolf will live with the lamb …
and a little child will lead them.

– Isaiah 2:4,11:6

Go in peace to love and to serve;
WE WILL SEEK PEACE AND PURSUE IT.

*– From the closing responses of the
Morning service in Iona Abbey*

CONTENTS

AT HOME

INTRODUCTION

'Well, I've dropped so many bombs into other people's lives, I wouldn't know where to start,' said Chaz, in the homeless shelter, in Ottawa, one night. He couldn't sleep and was up smoking. We were playing cards to make it through to morning, Crazy 8s. It was 20 below outside and the world seemed frozen-dead: through the window, moonlight on an expanse of city wasteland and a couple winter-blasted trees, like a painting by Paul Nash. In the distance, the sound of trucks working at clearing another impasse of snow and ice.

We were talking about making peace in our lives: you got talking about all sorts of things at the shelter in the middle of the night.

I confessed that things were still not right with an ex, and maybe never would be. Or maybe time would pass and things would just naturally resolve themselves …

'Yeah, maybe,' said Chaz … 'It's just – you know watching the news, like tonight – Iraq: all the bombs and craziness, all the bullets and bombs in Iraq, landmines in Afghanistan: sometimes I look at that and think: *that's what I've done to other people.* I've never shot anyone, or even beaten anyone up bad, really, but I've sure dropped some bombs and bullets and landmines into the heart of other people's lives … My wife, family, friends … Guess they've dropped some in mine too … Sometimes I just get angry … Mostly it makes me sad … Guess we all gotta talk someday.'

Chaz blew on his hands and huddled closer to the heater; there was the smell of coffee reaching in from the kitchen: my eternally sunny shift-mate whistling and brewing up some hope.

'And the war just goes on and on, you know? ... My son's the same. Though I don't really see him. Saw him for the first time in a long time a few weeks ago. That was good ... And my old man, he was the same.'

Chaz was seeing his social worker and trying to cut down on his drinking. And not doing coke. He was thinking of going for counselling too.

I'm not sure how he did in the end. He came back to the shelter after having his own place for a bit, then I never saw him again. But I always remember his words about dropping bombs and bullets and landmines into the heart of other people's lives, and our middle-of-the-frozen-night conversation about the cycle of violence, and peacemaking.

George lived in the same night shelter. George had fought in World War Two and in Korea.

When I asked him about fighting in the wars once, he was silent. Then said, '... I don't like to talk about it, son.'

The only thing he'd ever really say about it, after a bottle of Chinese cooking wine, or in the middle of the frozen night, sitting huddled by the glowing heart of the space-heater, was:

'Son ... I just don't understand why so many good people died and *I* lived. There must be a reason ... I can't come to peace with that.'

When the Iraq war started – God, so many years ago now – he knew I was going to demos on Parliament Hill and asked if he could come along.

'Sure!' I said.

And there he was: a soldier and veteran of the streets standing with a crowd of fresh-faced, placard- and megaphone-waving university students.

On an evening of a debate and key vote in Parliament, we held a vigil on the steps of the Peace Tower. Lit white candles and gently sang 'All we are saying is give peace a chance' … An MP came striding by, and George stopped him. He was a veteran of the Second World War and of Korea, he told the MP, and gave him his rank, regiment and Veterans Affairs number.

'My brothers and friends, who were killed in those wars, or who died later, would want me to tell you this war is wrong.'

Then he told him that his marriage had failed because of the war. That he wasn't the person he should have been for his family because of it.

'Some come home wounded, missing arms and legs. Some come home crippled inside … You need to be able to live with yourself,' he told the MP, and looked him in the eye.

At first the politician looked taken aback; seemed jolted into reality. But then his face smoothed back into a sort of mask. He listened politely; stood erect with a ceremonial respect. And then thanked George and shook his hand, and hurried off on up the steps and into Parliament.

'That was totally *right on*,' one of the university students said. 'Wow!'

'Least you had your say, George,' I said.

'Men in suits sending little boys and girls to die,' said George.

We stopped on the way back to the shelter for a bottle of wine, and I helped him tie his shoes.

The Iraq war went on.

George's war went on, until he died of cirrhosis of the liver…

***

I'd like to think I'm a peaceful person. I grew up in the post-hippy fog of 1970s North America, where '60s casualties and lost prophets still trudged the highway trying to find a way to *'get back to the Garden'*. I imbibed the heady peace-and-love vibe with the pot smoke wafting from my big brother's bedroom. Inherited his album collection – the Beatles; Jimi Hendrix; Janis Joplin; Cream; Crosby, Stills, Nash and Young – when he hitched down to California looking for freedom and love, man: freedom from my parents, who had given him everything, including love. I'm 51 – and still have long hippy hair, although it's grey and thinning (like my ideals I think, sometimes). 'Almost cut my hair,' cautioned counter-culture guru David Crosby on *Déjà Vu* (side one, track three). Being a 'hippy' is part of how I define my (vague) roots. So I'd like to think I'm a peaceful person.

But it's easy to believe in and espouse peace and love after growing up in the affluence of post-war North America. I've never been to Vietnam. I just sang about it (years after the fact) – with passion. I've not had to fight, very much, or had big wars in life. So I've not really been pushed or tested. Well, not like some people.

So it's easy to edit an anthology about peace and reconciliation and put your name on it. But I'm no expert in peace and reconciliation. (I'm no expert in anything.) I'm often at war, and have no agenda for reconciling the divided sides of myself, which occasionally do make peace – in grace-filled moments of being and sharing, thank God. And, to me, that's life. But I do violence and damage to brothers and sisters in the confusion. *'I do not understand my own actions. For I do not do what I want, but I do the very thing I hate'* (Romans 7:15). I have my feuds and little wars. I haven't made peace with some people, and I *have* made peace with some people. The older I get, the less patient wisdom I seem to have in store – when I thought for certain I'd *gain* in its acquisition. I do my best, which is often not good enough. I'm a fragile, flawed human being in need of the forgiveness and grace flowing from the heart of God and hearts of other fellow fragile, flawed and beautiful human beings.

This book is simply 'my' small contribution to the *'ministry of peace and reconciliation'* (2 Corinthians 5:16–6:2): a book for personal and group reflection or for use in worship. May it help bring healing.

2014-2018 marks the centenary of the First World War: the *'war to end all wars'*, and many folk, communities and organisations have been commemorating that in different ways. 'Peace and reconciliation' was a recent yearly 'theme' of the Iona Community, and this book partly came out of that. Many contributors to the book are members, associates or friends of the Community, which, from its beginning, has been engaged in work for peace and reconciliation.

This is a book about *'the bombs and bullets and landmines we drop into the heart of other people's lives'* – and the many many good folk working for peace and reconciliation at home and abroad.

I'm conscious that I haven't covered every aspect or area of peacemaking here. I've done what I can.

Thank you to all the contributors. And thank you to everyone else who sent me material. I'm sorry I wasn't able to include it all.

Thank you to the Wild Goose team – Sandra Kramer, Jane Darroch Reilly, Alex O'Neill and Debbie White – for support and companionship.

Peace,

Neil

WORLD WAR ONE AND TWO:
TO END ALL WARS

COSTLY AND COURAGEOUS WITNESS

My mother once told me that when she left Leighton Church, Dunblane after a morning service in June 1915, someone said to her: 'Your father will be in trouble for preaching a sermon like that.' She was shocked and astonished. Her fourteen years had taught her that her father was a gentle scholarly minister who cared for his people. What had he said? The First World War public hysteria was at its height and all Germans were regarded as monsters. Rev. David Alexander decided that he could not connive with that. He declared from the pulpit that not all German people were bad and that he still valued his deep friendship with those who had been his companions as students at the University of Halle in the late 19th century. That simple, civilised and Christian statement was a costly and courageous witness that challenged the poison of the time.

Iain Whyte

THE RECONCILING POWER OF REVOLUTIONARY LOVE

On Sunday 9 August 1914, a few days after Britain declared war with Germany, a huge gathering assembled on Glasgow Green for a Peace Demonstration. The press did not see fit to cover the event, so it was left to *Forward* – the newspaper of the Independent Labour Party in Scotland – to report that a crowd of five thousand gathered *'to protest against the outbreak of war and the exploitation of the people's food supply by the profiteers who pose as patriots'.*[1] Organised by the ILP, the British Socialist Party and the Glasgow Peace Society, the protest attracted *'rebels of every kind, from mild peace advocates to the wildest of revolutionaries'.* Truly, those women and men in Scotland and other warring lands, who stood against the overwhelming tide of jingoistic patriotic fervour to resist war and work for peace, were a rare collection of rebels and revolutionaries. They included feminists who believed that the struggles for women's rights and against war were inseparable: women like Chrystal Macmillan from Edinburgh. A committed internationalist, she was at the heart of a remarkable women's movement calling for conflict resolution by conciliation and arbitration. Chrystal helped to organise the Women's Peace Congress at The Hague in April 1915, and became secretary of the Women's International Committee for Permanent Peace (from 1919 the Women's International League for Peace and Freedom – still campaigning today). On its behalf, and under extremely adverse circumstances, she travelled across Europe seeking opportunities to meet with national leaders as advocate for the WICPP peace by negotiation proposals.[2]

Helen Crawfurd was involved in the Scottish wing of this feminist campaign – but she also wanted women to risk more direct confrontation and propaganda for peace. A militant suffragette and Christian socialist, in the summer of 1916 she mobilised war-weary working-class women in

Glasgow into a grassroots Women's Peace Crusade, organised through stairheid meetings and mass rallies and by 1917 spreading like wildfire across industrial centres in Scotland, Wales and the north of England. Helen and her allies (all veterans of the women-led 1915 Glasgow rent strikes) were adept at using dramatic direct action to protest: not only against the slaughter of war, but also the censorship, hardship and exploitation of living in a militarised State. When Glasgow Corporation refused their request to receive a peace deputation, WPC members gathered in George Square, held banners high and raised their voices in noisy opposition to the war. Helen and Agnes Dollan *'managed, by fair means or foul, to gain entry to the City Chambers and as the meeting of the Corporation got under way, they showered the councillors with anti-war leaflets'.*[3] They were arrested and found guilty of breaching the peace! Helen Crawfurd was one of the acknowledged leaders and most powerful speakers of the socialist anti-war movement, which was particularly strong in Scotland. Along with Red Clydeside comrades like John MacLean and Willie Gallacher, she was imprisoned for her political resistance to the war machine, and her bold advocacy of international solidarity.

Opposition to the First World War was not just politically motivated: for thousands, resisting violent conflict and killing of fellow human beings was a matter of religious and moral conscience. European imperial expansion, with Britain leading the way, had been justified in part as the benevolent extension of Christian civilisation. And Churches on both sides of the conflict were enthusiastic recruiting agents for the war effort. Clergymen preached the glory of fighting and sacrifice for a righteous cause, and extolled the war as God's purifying fire. As one Scottish Churchman proclaimed, *'It is the hour for a true man to feel for his sword.'*[4] But many Christians were profoundly disturbed by the paradox of prosecuting a bloody war of attrition in the name of a gospel of peace.

William Marwick was the son of a Presbyterian minister and a student at Edinburgh University when war broke out. He was shocked at the prevailing pro-war attitude in his own denomination (although his own convictions were influenced by a few pacifist ministers of an older gener-ation) and turned to Edinburgh Unitarians and Quakers for support and encouragement when he appealed against conscription in 1916, and was imprisoned as a conscientious objector. By then he was a committed Christian pacifist – a position his pro-war minister described '*as being the result of careful study in economic and political science backed by intense spiritual conviction*'. At his Court Martial, William maintained '*in no case can I recognise the legitimacy of an external human authority which demands the absolute direction of my conscience. I am convinced that the only way to eliminate war is to refuse to become an accomplice in it. Consid-ering military force to be futile and immoral, I must decline to take up arms in any cause whatsoever.*'[5] Over 16,000 British men refused military orders as conscientious objectors – and many paid a heavy price for the courage of their convictions.

Although Christian pacifists and conscientious objectors were a despised and persecuted minority during the war, the mainstream Churches in Britain and Germany had been engaging in initiatives to build interna-tional friendship and understanding right up until the outbreak of war. In August 1914, one hundred and fifty church representatives gathered for a peace conference in Konstanz, Germany. The meeting had to be aban-doned after one day, but from it emerged a World Alliance for Promoting International Friendship through the Churches (later incorporated into the World Council of Churches).

How quickly were those good intentions overwhelmed by the tsunami of paranoia, hostility and slaughter which engulfed Europe. But at Cologne station two of the participants, British Quaker Dr Henry Hodgkin and Friedrich Siegmund-Schultze, pacifist chaplain to the German Kaiser, believing that the bonds of Christian love transcended all national boundaries, vowed that they would refuse to sanction war or violence and that they would sow the seeds of peace and love no matter what the future might bring. As they bade farewell, they agreed that they were *'one in Christ and can never be at war'*.

Out of this vow the Fellowship of Reconciliation was born. In the final days of 1914, Hodgkin helped organise a conference in Cambridge for British Christians who shared his pacifist convictions. George Lansbury, Richard Roberts, Leyton Richards and Maude Royden were among the 128 present. They agreed that their concern went far beyond protest, or simply the absence of war. As Christians, they were called by God to live in fellowship, and to seek reconciliation in every aspect of life. In other words, their work and witness was to seek a new social order, breaking down barriers of violence, suspicion and hatred through *'the art and practice of turning enemies into friends'*. As the title of a FOR-published series of books and pamphlets on religious peacemaking suggested, this was 'The Christian Revolution'. During the First World War the Fellowship gave spiritual, emotional and practical support to the growing number of people who refused conscription on the grounds of conscience. William Marwick was a member, and attended weekly FOR meetings with fellow COs in Wakefield Work Centre. Membership grew steadily, and by 1917 there were 7000 in branches around Britain. An American FOR came into being in 1915 when Hodgkin visited the United States. In 1919 representatives from a dozen countries met in Holland and established the network soon to be known as the International Fellowship of Reconciliation (IFOR), which now has branches and groups in all five continents. George MacLeod served as IFOR President 1965-69, and over the years many other Iona Community members and associates have been deeply involved in the Fellowship, as staff members, officers and activists.

A century after that 'war to end all wars', let us celebrate the passionate rebels and revolutionaries who were not passivists, but believed in the reconciling power of revolutionary love. Women and men who had courage to test the possibility and practice of non-violent resistance to war, injustice and exploitation. For as Garth MacGregor (Professor of Divinity and Biblical Criticism at Glasgow University and leading FOR theologian of pacifism) wrote: *'The Christian must learn to live not as a baffled idealist but as a rebel against the world as it is.'*

Lesley Orr

NOTES:
1. *Forward*, Saturday, 15 August 1914
2. www.wilpfinternational.org
3. *Glasgow Herald*, 14 December 1917
4. *Life and Work*, 1916, 'Conscience and the War', by a Scottish Churchman, p.13
5. W.H. Marwick papers, Liddle Collection, Leeds University Library

PRAYERS FROM THE TRENCHES

The years 2014-2018 mark the centenary of World War One, when humanity discovered the horrors of modern mechanised warfare. At the Somme in 1916, a million men were killed or wounded. The war left a tragic legacy – redrawing the world map, awakening conflict in the Middle East, fuelling dangerous forms of nationalism and leaving unanswered the deaths of a million Armenian men, women and children.

In the 21st century, we still are fighting the conflict touched off by the assassination of an Austrian nobleman in 1914. So, as the world reflects on the fears in those trenches, it is important to remember the hopes and prayers as well: they echo to this day.

– Benjamin Pratt

Whisper down the trenches

Morning's dim light
shall see us scrambling from
this muddy trench
up slimy ladders
into the numbing noise of
bugles, bagpipes, flags flapping,
mortars and bombs bursting,
machine guns racketing and
screams of men crying for help,
calling for their mothers
with their final breaths.

Sunday after Sunday, we hear
God would never abandon us,
even in Hell.
Even in Hell?
Hell is here, Lord.
Make yourself known!

We were taught God is all-powerful,
all-loving, but –
I am not feeling your power.
I am not feeling your presence.
I am not feeling your love.
I am in the trenches.
I need you here.

If you are Lord –
if you are in the trenches –
drown the noise,
whisper tenderly in my ears.
Come down
through these trenches of Hell.
Whisper in each ear.
Like a mother, hold us to your breast;
calm our night terrors.

Whisper,
whisper,
Lord.
Quiet
the frightening noise.

Whisper
your presence, Lord.
Whisper
your love
like a comforting mother.
Whisper,
whisper,
whisper.

Tunneller's prayer

I am a miner.
I know the sound of the whistle
that calls me into the cold, dark shaft.
I know the sound of pick against rock,
sledge against support beam.
I've mined for coal to heat homes,
stoke factory furnaces.
I've mined for salt to preserve and season food.

Now I'm a tunneller carving like a mole to
plant explosives deep in the earth under
enemy lines to kill men I do not know.
I'm a warrior, waging war from the deep, dark depths
of Hell.

Bombs burst on the battlefield above.
I shudder as the
earth shakes, dust and stone shower down.
Each bomb rattles my soul.

I pray this will not be my grave.
I want my canary to keep singing.
I want to see the sun and blue sky,
to hear the blackbird squawk,
to feel the warmth of my wife,
to bounce and laugh with my son
on my knee,
to dig coal to heat homes,
to live and sing,
to plough my field, grow my crops,
to plant seeds of peace.

Benjamin Pratt

DEAD MAN'S PENNY

A second cousin e-mailed me to ask about a war memorial plaque for a Patrick Power. 'Who was he?' he asked.

He had the plaque and my people the story. Patrick was the youngest son of a widow, and turned eighteen in the summer of 1914. Like thousands of others, he followed the recruiting posters to enlist in the Connaught Rangers. They were young men seeking adventure for a few months, away from the dullness of Galway. Meanwhile, every girl admires a uniform. They went to be the cannon fodder of Flanders.

The training was brief and basic before they left for the trenches. Perhaps they were already there that first December of the war, when peace and sense reigned for a few days in a truce kept by foot-soldiers wiser than their masters. They had all hoped to be home for Christmas.

In Galway his mother was desperate. She wrote to her eldest son John, twice Patrick's age, away in the rear lines. 'Get him out of there!' she pleaded.

Patrick went to meet his brother, but found there a stranger who told him not to worry: his big brother would get him home safe. Patrick, fresh from burying comrades blown to pieces, turned on him in fury. By the time John arrived, it was too late for Patrick to listen. He went back that night to the trenches *'where the real men are'*. Five weeks later, he was dead. The Great War was ten months old.

It was a small family tragedy repeated ten million times. Perhaps his mother was the widow who came forward in another Galway recruitment drive. 'Will sending more men to the front,' she asked, 'bring me back my son?' She was escorted from the scene.

Patrick's plaque was in dark bronze, modelled on the penny of the time, but much larger. One side is dominated by Britannia, but not seated in grandeur; she stands head bowed, holding a laurel wreath over the dead soldier's name. The lion by her side is also bowed in grief. But far down at the base, a smaller lion defeats the Prussian eagle.

Each plaque is unique, carrying only the name of the deceased, with no age or rank or regiment. In a rare outburst of democracy, all were deemed equal in death. For every man who died, and some women too, this round bronze plaque was struck: a 'dead man's penny' for the relatives.

The reverse is blank, for these were meant for display. But Patrick's was never displayed.

It was struck in 1920. By then John could never come home, for Ireland's War for Independence meant there was no longer any welcome for a man from the British Army. He kept his brother's brief story, and a widowed emigrant sister took charge of the plaque and hid it away, while the mother lost sight of both her sons.

By 1920 Patrick's bones had been moved from his makeshift grave. They have lain since in a French cemetery. On 1 June 2015, the centenary of his death, my cousin visited.

First published anonymously in French in 1911 is a prayer said by millions since, attributed to the medieval saint Francis of Assisi, who had the courage to turn away from a life of fighting:

Lord, make me an instrument of your peace.
Where there is hatred, let me sow love;
where there is injury, pardon;
where there is doubt, faith;
where there is despair, hope;
where there is darkness, light;
and where there is sadness, joy.

O Divine Master, grant that I may not so much seek
to be consoled as to console;
to be understood as to understand;
to be loved as to love.

For it is in giving that we receive;
it is in pardoning that we are pardoned;
and it is in dying that we are born to eternal life.

Rosemary Power

GLIMPSES OF YOUR PRESENCE

Encompassing God, it's hard to fathom
that in the midst of the hell of war,
the muck and stench of the trenches,
exhausted men ceased from battle
to meet each other to play football.

Other stories tell of Easter:
gifts of decorated eggs
rolled into each other's foxholes;
and the singing of Christmas hymns
across barbed wire and ravaged earth.

Everlasting God,
these glimpses of your presence,
in the midst of war and wounding,
reflect your deeper self in the heart
of everyone –
in the very air between us.

Turn us round to face you
where we least expect to find you;
guide our steps towards
the unity of our beginnings.
Amen

Yvonne Morland

UNCLE OSWALD

I was eight years old when my Uncle Oswald was killed by a sniper at the Siege of Calais in 1940. He was my favourite uncle and it was my first experience of grief. The 2nd Battalion of the Kings Royal Rifle Corps (KRRC) was intended to hold Calais to slow down the German advance on Dunkirk, where over 300,000 servicemen and women were rescued. Those left at Calais were captured.

70 years later, a blog was written about me by Isobel Williams as I supported the OCCUPY encampment at St Paul's Cathedral in October 2011. I talked about my childhood and Uncle Oswald. The blog was read by Greg Manko, a teacher in Toronto, Canada. He e-mailed Isobel: *'I am trying to find the family of someone mentioned in your blog of 11/11/11 (Remembrance Day). I have a war service medal issued to an Oswald Segar-Owen that I would like to try to return to the family. One of his family members, Rev. Paul Nicolson, was featured in your blog from that day. I am trying to find contact information for him.'*

Greg and I corresponded and he sent the medal to my home in Tottenham. It was a General Service Medal with a Palestine bar. My brother Guy and I took it to the Greenjackets Museum in Winchester where KRRC memorabilia is displayed. How the medal found its way to the collection of Greg's late father in Canada remains a mystery.

Prayer (on John 17:11–23)

O Lord, let your love for us
give us all such love for you
that we may love each other
and be one.

May we be completely one,
consecrated in truth
and protected from evil.

Share your joy with us to the full,
so the world may know you
and be healed.

Come, Holy Spirit, and let us be one,
in our Lord Jesus Christ.
Amen

Paul Nicolson

MY TWO GRANDFATHERS

In the spring of 2014 I visited the beautiful Schallaburg castle in Lower Austria to see an exhibition about the First World War. The exhibition was special as the organisers had chosen to present this global disaster in the life stories of 25 very ordinary men and women, who had struggled through the Great War as combatants on deadly fronts or with keeping up life 'back home'. There they were: soldiers who had previously ploughed fields, and nurses who had come straight from a classroom; engineers firing heavy artillery, and doctors trying to deal with the terrible wounds these weapons inflicted. There was an Aboriginal prisoner of war, and a Jewish war correspondent from Galicia; there were individuals from British, French and German colonies in Africa, drawn into a faraway fight for hegemony, and Americans pulled into the war's decisive phase without knowing much about the history of Europe's struggling empires …

As I moved through the disturbing display of the suffering we are able to inflict on each other, I was sadly reminded that it was all closer to me than I was prepared to admit. My two grandfathers had fought in the Great War: my German grandfather in the battles of the Somme, and my Austrian grandfather on the Isonzo front. As they weren't officers, no records of them were kept in the military archives. Like millions of others they served and put their lives on the line. They were fortunate to survive, but were strangely broken after. They would never talk about the war: haunted by the traumatic experience of having killed and of having seen comrades being killed.

Growing up after World War Two, my brothers and I weren't really aware that our grandfathers had fought against the British, French and Italians, and that these people had once been our 'enemies'. We went to Italy for holidays; our parents taught us to love not only the beaches but also the people, and their deep appreciation for art and beauty. My mother learned Italian to be able to speak with the locals – and to bargain in the many markets! Later, we went to Britain to improve our English, and to France to learn something in the museums of Paris. My best friend during my student days was a Welsh girl, so I learned early on to respect and appreciate difference.

Today, ever more young people participate in cultural exchanges, like the EU-based Erasmus programme. One of my nieces studied in France, and is convinced: *'You can never forget the life you have shared together.'* Young people study and work abroad, marry and experience a new mixing of cultures and lifestyles that does not cling to the past, but rather asks what the common future should look like.

Peace is a quality of relationships; it needs to be practised and nurtured. It is a process that requires a stable environment, a framework, time and money (still infinitely less money than our assorted defence budgets!). To create such an environment was the declared goal of the European Union and its forerunners, and to the extent that it has become unimaginable that European countries should fight against each other again, the EU is a peace project and a successful one.

Still, peace is not something we can own: we have to keep pursuing it. Because it may well be that we have simply shifted aggression to another 'other': that it's no longer my Austrian grandfather fighting the Italians, or the 'Tommies' fighting the 'Huns', but all of us fighting the Muslims, the terrorists, and the asylum seekers landing on our coasts and islands.

Reconciliation is about creating a common future, in spite of the harsh memories of the past, and working for it, together with all – really with all!

Reinhild Traitler-Espiritu

YITZCHAK ZIEMAN (1920-2007): FROM PERSECUTION TO RECONCILIATION

I got to know Yitzchak in 1977 in a workshop called 'Crisis in Groups and Individual Crisis'. Later, we co-led workshops. When I visited him in New York, and later, in 2000 when he stayed with us – while giving some very moving talks to my congregation – he told me his life story:

In 1920, Lithuania was a small independent country. People got along well. Among Christians of different denominations and Jews there seemed to be tolerance and no discrimination. In the villages people lived together peacefully. Children went to the same schools and neighbours helped one another.

Yitzchak was the eldest of six children. In 1939, he joined the army to fight the Nazis. When they occupied his country, he got the sudden urge to go home to his village. But on the way he met a woman he knew: 'Don't go home,' she said. 'The villagers are killing all the Jews … All of your family are dead. And they will kill you too.' Yitzchak was shocked. Even his little sister had been killed?

He fled to Russia to fight the Germans, but as a Jew had no chance. He was arrested and sent to a gulag, where he nearly died of hunger. A young female doctor saved him. She managed to keep him in the infirmary until he was better and then helped him to escape.

His next memory was of being in a small town – and the smell of freshly baked bread. He walked into a bakery, and was handed a piece of bread. Then, suddenly, he turned, and saw a beautiful young woman, and so *'started to become a person again'*: a young man who was alive.

He travelled to Greece, where, again, he fought the Nazis. By the end of the war he was in hiding in Poland.

In May 1945, he came to Munich, where the American Occupation Services engaged him to work with Jews who had survived the concentration camps, as he spoke many languages. He had to listen to many terrible experiences. The task was too hard. After some time he ended up in a clinic.

When he recovered, he made the decision to become a psychotherapist – to be able to work with individuals who had been through the worst experiences – and obtained a visa to study in America.

In the U.S. he met other survivors of the Holocaust, like Ruth Cohn from Berlin. Together they developed a new way of working with groups called Theme-centred Interaction (TCI), to aid in better understanding, e.g. between black and white Americans, or different tribes and clans – a terrible mass killing like the Holocaust should never happen again.

In 1970, Ruth came back to Europe, bringing Yitzchak and other psychotherapists with her to help lead workshops and conferences. Yitzchak himself began to work on the theme: 'Jews and the children of the Nazis: what do we have to share which will help us to understand each other better?'

In 1980 he married, a German woman; and travelled to Israel as part of the 'Peace Now' movement. He wanted to work with Israelis and Palestinians, but was not welcome in the country. This must have been a very difficult experience for him as he did not want to talk about it.

What impressed me most about Yitzchak was his modesty when he spoke about his life, and his eagerness to listen to the experiences of others, especially Germans. Very late in life he was again able to sing the Yiddish songs from his childhood, part of a culture nearly extinguished by the Nazis.

I learned of Yitzchak's death when I was volunteering as an Ecumenical Accompanier in Palestine and Israel. His personality has encouraged me never to give up hope and to continue networking for peace and reconciliation.

Elisabeth Christa Miescher

'TO END ALL WARS': A WEEK ON IONA

'Where on earth would you get such a mixture of rich experiences: role play, craft, graffiti – and worship in between?' ...

'Unbearable ... fun ... constructive ideas of something to do' ...

'I never imagined I would be singing "Pack up your troubles in your old kit bag" at the top of my voice in the Chapter House of Iona Abbey!' ...

These are some of the comments from the participants in the 'To End All Wars' week at the Abbey and MacLeod Centre in June 2014.

I led the week with Steve Whiting, a long-time colleague and friend working for Quaker Peace and Social Witness in London. Obviously our focus for the week was the commemoration of the pain, suffering and sacrifice of people during the First World War, but also included reflections on all wars, and folk's endeavours to work for peace. It was necessarily a hard topic and some of it was indeed 'unbearable', but, as is the way in Iona, our programme was very varied and creative. We studied and discussed some pretty harrowing first-hand material from diaries and letters from World War One; we participated in a hilarious role play which revealed a great deal about disinformation, propaganda and the many dilemmas of conflict; we sang songs of war and peace; and we listened to a fascinating presentation on the effects of WWI on composers and musicians. And, of course – we talked, argued and discussed. All this amid the beauty of Iona in the best of summer weather. As one participant said: 'The island itself creates safety and the possibility of being open and vulnerable.'

And it was this openness and vulnerability which enabled one of the finest sessions of the week. On the Wednesday evening we gathered round very informally in the Mac common room, seated on cushions and chairs, for a storytelling session. There was no set order, but as each personal story or memory of war was told, others followed naturally and a pattern emerged. People shared their experiences at a very deep level and we were all profoundly moved.

For our last day, we moved on to feedback on the week, and practical suggestions for peacemaking, and ended up with a list of '15 Action Points for Peace'.

It was obvious from the feedback that the most significant experience for all of us had been the deeply personal sharing of stories. One after the other, phrases from the feedback session reflected certain themes: 'conversations', 'trust', 'inner dynamic', 'mixed international group', 'learning from each other', and, again and again: 'building relationships'.

I realise, now, that I had gone to the week with an agenda: I am an impatient, impulsive and often hasty activist and I think I was looking for some sort of blueprint of radical action 'to end all wars' (what an optimist!); but what the group came up with in their list of action points seemed to me to be rather vague and fluffy. So I tucked it away for future reference.

Then, when I went home, I came across an article on 'Practical peacemaking' in the Quaker magazine, *The Friend*. In it, the writer laid out five principles of peacemaking:

Peacemaking is non-violent.
Peacemaking is inclusive.
Peacemaking is a process.
Peacemaking is a practical activity.
Peacemaking is a relationship.

The author went on to say: '*Managing conflict peacefully and sustainably means transforming relationships at all levels of social contact, from our close personal relationships to the sharing of our planetary home.*' [1]

It was time to fish the comments down from the shelf. And there it all was – phrase after phrase echoing the theme of the article: that building relationships is the key component of building peace and good relations. There was nothing fluffy about these action points – the challenge was to carry them out. Which is why it was important that, on our last day on Iona, we spent time in silence writing a promise to ourselves to find some way, however small, of working where we are 'to end all wars'.

15 Action Points for Peace
(from the 'To end all wars' week, Iona, 2014)

1. Try to meet the enemy: '*If you want to make peace with your enemy, you must work with your enemy, then he/she becomes your partner*' (Nelson Mandela). Sitting down and listening to each other.

2. Make the decision to go to war more democratic, with the approval of Parliament required, or through referendum. To be effective this will require involving a higher proportion of the population in politics and voting, and pushing politicians.

3. Adopting measures to address growing economic inequality, both within and between nations.

4. Do much more with children and in schools to develop self-awareness, empathy and compassion: reference to 'Roots of Empathy' programme by Mary Gordon in Canada (www.rootsofempathy.org).

5. Address attitudes to war and develop empathy and understanding for each other. Change adversarial systems in UK Parliament, courts and develop cooperative systems.

6. Everyone should become more aware of the implications of climate change for the world. We need to take individual actions to minimise our personal use of natural resources. Use Christian Ecology link: www.greenchristian.org.uk

7. Remembrance services must avoid any glorification of war – by acknowledging our responsibility for the evil of war (penitential element in the service), by setting up realistic church displays and offering red and white poppies.

8. Christians and others can encourage friendships and contact with local people who are different. Interfaith forums can be very useful here. Welcome should be offered to groups such as Travellers.

9. We can all do a report for our own church magazine on the peace week. In doing intercessions we can select and read prayers on peace issues or race. We can speak up in church meetings and councils.

10. UN peacekeeping forces need to be properly resourced, supported and trained.

11. History books need to be rewritten!

12. We could suggest that local newspapers seek stories from soldiers; perhaps that schools ask for war stories.

13. We need to do more to show the power of non-violence to bring about social change.

14. We need to do more to keep memories of war alive, through stories of survivors and families, through documents and archives.

15. All this needs to begin with ourselves: with our determination to become better human beings and to build a better world.

Helen Steven

NOTE:
1. Author unknown

ON 'MEEK REFUSAL'

August 2014 was my first visit to Iona in exactly ten years and my first stay on the island – what a privilege to spend it with Community members, staff and volunteers. I had two roles for Community Week: one was to facilitate the morning sessions as we explored the topic of our local communities being places of spiritual activism – the other was to have fun and explore the island!

One of my highlights from the former experience was our conversation about what I call 'meek refusal' and some others call 'non-violent resistance' or 'non-compliance'. I loved hearing people's stories about the examples children give us of 'meek resistance'. Some of them had us creased with laughter.

If you've ever looked after children – your own or those of someone else – you have probably witnessed meek refusal at its most effective. Children are experts in non-violent resistance. They have to be, since anyone who gets between them and another biscuit is going to be bigger and stronger. Here are some favourite examples that I've collected from friends:

Cuddling and refusing to let go

'I love you, Mummy – even when you're cross!'

The general art of faffing plus wanting to do something entirely different to what's on offer!

Weeing himself in awkward places ... lying on the floor howling – sorry, lamenting

Distracting me with random requests for a story

Non-violent resistance to going to bed: needing extra kisses, stating random fears that need resolving, wanting more stories/songs/prayers …

My younger daughter has always ignored anyone saying anything she didn't want to hear … but open a packet of chocolate buttons under a duvet at the other end of the house, and she is there in seconds!

My daughter frequently uses the 'sit-in' technique or the 'make yourself go really floppy and slippery' one.

Silence; refusing to eat

'He picked up chocolate that he knew he shouldn't have, sat down and announced: "Don't worry, Mum, I'm eating it on the naughty stair."'

And just so that you know that children aren't the only ones with the gift, here's a quote from a member of the Christian Peacemaker Teams (CPT):

I used non-violent resistance against a toddler … does that count? I was visiting some friends during a break in my CPT training. I went upstairs to read the littlest one a bedtime story and mummy came up too. I was sitting on the bed with baby … and the book. Mummy said, 'Can I sit down too?' Baby answers 'NO!' So, I sat down on the floor with mummy until baby could agree that there was space on the bed for everyone. I suppose it was really solidarity with parents. Don't mess with CPT, kids.[1]

Meek refusal has been an important tool for industrial struggles and political resistance throughout history. So it is no surprise that it turns up in the biblical tradition too.

Take the Hebrew midwives in the Exodus saga, for example. The Hebrew people have been domesticated as a slave caste within a powerful empire:

forced into back-breaking labour and political impotence. The ruler of the empire becomes concerned that a new generation of Hebrews may get political and rise up against him. So he orders the Hebrew midwives to kill all newborn baby boys on arrival. The midwives seem to have two options: follow the orders or protest them. But they choose a third option, meek refusal.

To be meek is to show restraint in one's actions. Meekness allows for a measured and therefore more productive response to oppression. This is why Jesus said that *'the meek shall inherit the earth'* (Matthew 5). Jesus knew that those who can restrain themselves from merely reacting to someone else's agenda will find a way to have their hunger for justice more completely satisfied.

So what do the midwives do? Well, at first they just don't comply: they let the babies live. But the emperor is not going to sit back and watch his orders ignored. He is both a man and a God and they are only women and of the slave caste. He demands an explanation.

The midwives said to [the emperor], 'Because the Hebrew women are not like the [local] women; for they are vigorous and give birth before the midwife comes to them.' So God dealt well with the midwives; and the people multiplied and became very strong. And because the midwives feared God, he gave them families. (Exodus 1:19–21, NRSV)

He gets an explanation: the Hebrew women are too strong and give birth before the midwife can arrive. Now tell me, Mr Emperor: what do you know about gynaecology then? Care to contradict? I didn't think so. No doubt this explanation would not have washed with the emperor but it stood nonetheless as the barefaced but sidestepping resistance of violence and oppression. The Hebrew people were not yet in a position to escape completely from the grip of empire so they had to try every trick in the book to work the system just to survive for now.

In 1941 the Nazi-controlled government in Norway tried to force professionals to join up with fascist-affiliated bodies; they met with meek refusal on all fronts. The athletics groups disbanded, unions refused and forty-three professional bodies signed an open and joint declaration against compulsory membership in the Nazi Party. This resistance was met by violent recriminations, prison sentences and repression that triggered *'mass resignations from the organisations and, far from weakening them, gave them new vitality'.*[2] Schools and churches joined in with their own resistance; bishops and teachers setting the example of public refusal were sacked but continued to publicly defy the Nazis, leading to a massive climbdown from the fascist regime.

Throughout Europe, civilian resistance saved more lives than military combat could ever hope to lay claim to. This was especially so in those regions where Jewish people were fully integrated into wider society.

Despite the overwhelming success of meek refusal compared to Allied military force, cultural rituals in Britain perpetuate the state-sponsored myth of redemptive violence. This is because our governments know that if people got wise to the power of meek refusal, their rulers, elected and otherwise, would not be able to oppress, exploit or ignore them any more.

Keith Hebden

NOTES:
1. A member of the CPT team in Canada
2. *Unarmed Against Hitler: Civilian Resistance in Europe*, 1939-1943, Jacques Semelin, Praeger, 1993

GEORGE

An old story of mine, but one still worth telling, I think (Ed.)

I met George when I was going to college and working part-time at a shelter for homeless men. When I wasn't busy, and he was free, we'd sit and talk together, about art and classical music. As a young man, George had studied oil painting. He'd wanted to learn to draw like the old masters, he told me. He loved the art of portraiture especially, and had dreamed of, just once, capturing a face so that it 'mirrored the soul'.

At first it seemed a little surprising to be talking about art and music in the cacophony of a night shelter, surrounded by bare, nicotine-yellow walls and ugly, orange linoleum scarred with cigarette burns.

I'd heard that George had been a soldier, too, that he'd fought at Normandy and in the Desert campaign, later again in Korea, but when I asked him about that period of his life, he said he didn't like to talk about it.

Once when Tommy was having a seizure, and lay writhing on the cold floor like he'd been shot, I glanced up and saw George. He gazed down at Tommy and kept shaking his head; it was like he was away some place else. His face expressed infinite pity.

Blood drooled from the corner of Tommy's mouth; his body kept flailing and churning. 'Gonna be alright, Tom,' said George. Tommy roiled and writhed, his boyish, trenched face contorted, tortured-looking.

George handed me his suit jacket, balled-up for underneath Tommy's head. I tried to keep Tommy over on his side between attacks; with a tender, sore, caressing voice, George told Tommy that he was going to be all right, that he was just going to see the nurses.

'Just goin' to see the nurses,' the crowd of tough, scared men started up in a chorus. 'Tommy's just going to see the nurses.' 'Luck-y.' 'Some nice ones there, I'll bet ya.' 'Oh yeah, for sure.' 'Be alright now, Tommy.' 'Tommy, be alright.' And, finally, the ambulance screamed up with a stretcher the paramedics rolled Tommy on to like a bag of loose sticks.

My colleague Phil, who'd been working on the front line for years, and knew George better than anyone probably, said that George felt profound guilt for having survived the wars – that George couldn't understand why he'd lived when all his good friends, and so many other good people, had been blown away or left crippled for life, had been taken prisoner and tortured, had gone missing and never been found … He carried the question like a cross, Phil said. 'You see him alone sometimes, talking to himself, talking to God. Shouting at the heavens; praying for peace.'

A tabloid newspaper portrayed George as a dirty old drunk, on its front page one day. Some photojournalist shot him as he sat alone out on the front stoop of the shelter with a 'dead soldier' beside him. He looked like a poor, pathetic soul: dressed in a crumpled tweed jacket, bowed down by drink. The angle and light didn't do him justice, made his face look ugly and guttered. 'A Skid Row Alcoholic', the title underneath the picture read. There was a story concerning the growing number of homeless and the face of downtown. There was no report of him talking gently, humanly to Tommy as he lay writhing in hell, of the wars of liberation and absurdity he'd fought in through deserts and jungles and back streets; no mention that he had a wife and grown children somewhere, or of his dreams to become a fine artist who mirrored the soul.

No quote of him speaking knowledgeably, sensitively, passionately about the rich, beautiful, soaring music of Gustav Mahler.

The guys were mad. Somebody wanted to go down and teach the reporter a lesson. 'Give the poser a slashin'.'

Phil said it didn't surprise him. 'People have been painting him like that for ages now. Still hurt him though, I bet.'

George had one of the most beautiful faces I've ever seen. Sitting across from him one night, I told him that; I'd felt overwhelmed. He said thank you, that I was a gentleman.

It was hard to express with words. George's face was like grainy, grey rock, its features sculpted and etched by wind and rain, pocked and scarred by ice and snow; like an ancient landscape that had experienced fecund, young times of flowers; sudden rifts; slow, glacial change. George's face shone with the experience and wisdom of ages –

'Maybe that's what they mean,' said Phil. 'About suddenly seeing the face of Christ.'

Neil Paynter

LORD REDEEM US

In our damaged histories,
Lord, redeem us from our past.

In our willing acts of conflict,
Lord, lead us to seek peace.

In our divisions and extremism,
Lord, unite us with your love.

In our confusion, indecision,
Lord, steady us with your power.

In our muddled intentions,
Lord, enlighten us with your truth.
Amen

Yvonne Morland

TRIDENT: WHAT KIND OF FIRE?

GARDENERS FOR PEACE: PLANTING SEEDS OF HOPE

Our group is called the Gareloch Horticulturalists Non-violent Action Group (try sewing that onto a banner!) and of course there is a story behind the name. On November 9th, 1983 the women at Greenham Common urged peace groups to demonstrate at all U.S. bases around Britain. Our group joined others camping outside RNAD Glen Douglas, which has sinister bunkers in the hillside storing half the ammunition for the North Atlantic fleet. Three of us climbed the fence into the base and planted a rose. When the policeman arresting me asked what I had been doing, and I told him, 'Planting a rose', his face lit up and he asked: 'What kind of rose?' 'A peace rose, of course'; to which he commented: 'Regular bunch of gardeners, aren't you?' And so the name, it stuck, the Gareloch being where the subs are based. Planting things soon became our trademark, and our slogan is *'Let us plant seeds of hope'*.

Looking back over our activities, certain periods seem to have been times of frenetic involvement. The years between 1983 and 1987 were busy ones for the peace movement in general, and this was reflected in the high level of activity of the 'Gareloch Hortis'. We hired a bus to take us to the '4th July Independence from the US' blockade at Greenham; some of us travelled to London to participate in a prayer protest in the Central Lobby of the House of Commons … On April 4th, the anniversary of the death of Martin Luther King, following the theme 'I have a dream', seven of us entered the submarine base at Faslane and planted potatoes as a symbol of food for the hungry. Two of us went to prison as a result …

We will continue, in spite of it all, to plant seeds of hope.

Helen Steven, February 1993

BREACH OF THE PEACE

*We believe that God is present
in the darkness before dawn:
in the waiting and uncertainty
where fear and courage join hands,
conflict and caring link arms,
and the sun rises over barbed wire.*

*We believe in a with-us God,
who sits down in our midst
to share our humanity.*

*We affirm a faith
that takes us beyond the safe place:
into action, into vulnerability
and into the streets.*

*We commit ourselves to work for change
and put ourselves on the line;
to bear responsibility, take risks,
live powerfully and face humiliation;
to stand with those on the edge;
to choose life
and be used by the Spirit
for God's new community of hope.
Amen*

Written by two Iona Community members
following a demo at Faslane in 2001

In February 2001, I was one of a number of people who took part in a sit-down demonstration at Faslane Nuclear Submarine Base.

Along with others, I was arrested, and charged with Breach of the Peace for conducting myself in a disorderly manner – i.e. taking part in a Communion service and then sitting in the road!

At my trial in September, I made the following statement:

> *'Sitting on the road, and thereby breaking the law, is not how I would necessarily choose to spend a day in February, nor is it something I undertook lightly. In fact, however, I firmly believe I had no choice in the matter, and that for two reasons:*

> *'1. Trident is capable of destroying most of the northern hemisphere in ten minutes. Thirty million men, women and children would be wiped out in ten minutes, and the effect of radiation would make much of the earth uninhabitable. I, therefore, as a mother and a grandmother, would be failing my children and my grandchildren if I did not make a stand against it.*

> *'2. The cost of Trident is the equivalent of spending £30,000 a day since the birth of Christ. Is this what we, a so-called civilised society, really consider to be a responsible use of our money? I work in partnership with families living in poverty and social exclusion in Glasgow, and therefore would be failing these people, who I feel privileged to call my friends, if I did not make a stand against this obscene expenditure.'*

In March 2002 I was summoned to appear at a Means Enquiry Court in Glasgow for an outstanding fine of £150 as a result of the above arrest and charge. I refused to pay, and was offered a Supervised Attendance

Order, which I also refused, as I explained that I would find it very difficult to fulfil, due to work and other commitments. I was then sentenced to seven days in Cornton Vale Women's Prison in Stirling (which was reduced, for good behaviour, to a long weekend!).

Molly Harvey

FROM IONA ABBEY TO NUMBER 10: PILGRIMAGE FOR PEACE AND SOCIAL JUSTICE

Setting off from Iona at Pentecost, the Pilgrimage for Peace and Social Justice finished outside the door of Number 10 Downing Street on 20th July, 2013. The primary purpose of the pilgrimage was *'to focus national public attention on the government's intention to spend up to £100 billion renewing the UK's Trident nuclear weapons system, while continuing to slash NHS, education and social welfare budgets – including vital financial support for some of the country's most vulnerable and disadvantaged people'.*

As we made our way from one end of the country to another, we discovered that pilgrimage can be a listening exercise as well as a community-building one. As we walked, we talked: with each other and with the thousands of others we met on the way. These conversations on the way ranged from the most fleeting, to people sharing parts of their life-story very deeply with us. Talking can have a different quality when you're walking together.

We also distributed over 15,000 leaflets giving an outline of our convictions and inviting people to visit our website for further information – and to sign a petition calling on the government to scrap Trident.

The overwhelming majority of people we spoke to agreed with us, about both the immorality of Trident and the fact that it is complete madness to be planning to spend up to £100 billion on its replacement at the same time as making massive cuts in spending on public services, while using the argument that the austerity measures are necessary because the government simply doesn't have the money to maintain former levels of spending. Many people who had been unaware of that contradiction and injustice were shocked to discover it.

While we were walking, Trident was repeatedly in the news: there was a call for the Labour Party to revisit its position on Britain's nuclear weapons, the publication of the Lib Dems' review of the alternatives to the UK's current level of nuclear capacity, and President Obama announced his intention to reduce the U.S. nuclear arsenal by up to a third, in a speech he made in Berlin. Such is the power of pilgrimage!

But it did more than that. Over the weeks the core group of walkers – strangers to each other at the start – became a community, not without the usual challenges involved in that of course; not least because we were together 24/7: walking all day, cooking and eating together in the evenings and then sharing the floor of a communal space at night.

Living for nine weeks out of a medium-sized rucksack, with a bit of communal equipment in the back of a van, is a useful reminder of the time and energy freed up by living fairly simply.

Something else that was brought home to us very strongly was the value of hospitality – we received a lot of good hospitality, especially from Quaker meetings in many places. My vote for the best meeting house goes to Osmotherly: a little 17th-century building with an open fire, a bunkhouse where we could sleep in beds – and a supply of homemade organic clotted cream from one member's dairy farm! I was struck by the closeness between the Quaker Peace Testimony and the Iona Community's Justice and Peace Commitment, and by their long and honourable history of living it.

Sometimes complete strangers took us home, fed us, washed our dirty socks and underwear for us and gave us a bed for the night. My most unusual stopover was spent in a house which was home to a very voluble parrot!

And hospitality is very much a mutual exchange: good for both giver and receiver. A woman seeing us as she drove past on a very hot day, stopped, wound her window down – and handed us a punnet of washed and prepared strawberries!

A Church of Scotland minister who was awaiting the imminent birth of his eighth child, and who'd been busy cooking for his family – made enough soup for all us pilgrims too.

Someone visiting us at the end of one particularly wet day, arrived with a supply of tablet, all lovingly wrapped in little individual bags tied with ribbon …

Some of the highlights and memorable moments of the pilgrimage for me: Iona Abbey Warden Joanna Anderson's send-off in the cloisters on Iona, during which a blackbird sang his heart out from the top of the tower the whole time.

Sailing up the Gareloch on the maritime branch of the pilgrimage (one fairly small boat!) and seeing the full horrifying extent of Faslane Nuclear base from the water, including a surfaced submarine.

We left the Abbey cloisters on Whitsunday morning, and arrived outside the front door of 10 Downing Street with our petition two months later.

Journeying together certainly changed us. And we will never know what seeds it has planted in others, and where that growth may lead.

Margery Toller

EASTER ADDRESS AT FASLANE SUBMARINE BASE, APRIL 12, 2014

Good Friday draws nigh, and again we stand outside this nuclear submarine base at Faslane, gathered in this act of public worship, this Witness for Peace of Scottish Christians Against Nuclear Arms.

We stand – including Catholic Archbishop, Church of Scotland Convener, and me a Quaker – drawn from the folds of many different denominations, the underlying undivided Christian Church that prays: 'Thy kingdom come.' Not Caesar's kingdom come, but God's; and so Pontius Pilate asked Jesus, 'Are you a king, then?' To which the Prince of Peace replied: 'King is your word.' And he spoke unto Pilate of non-violence, saying: 'My kingdom is not of this world. If it was, my followers would fight' (John 18:36–37).

Likewise, when the disciple cut off the ear of the high priest's servant, Jesus disarmed him, saying: 'Put away your sword, Peter … No more of this!' (John 18:11; Luke 22:51). Why? Because violence destroys our ability to hear one another. Christ healed the ear and healed our hearing, therefore Easter asks us: can we hear the deeper whisperings of the Cross? The Cross of wood and nails encircled with a crown of thorns that stood upon a green hill far away. The Cross of monstrous hulls and thermonuclear warheads surrounded by a barbed-wire fence that is this Trident missile base today.

The Bible claims that Christ came 'to give his life, as a ransom' (Mark 10:45; Matthew 20:28; 1 Timothy 2:6), and so, to a central question of the Cross: Who – is the ransomer of souls?

Throughout the first millennium the church's main answer was the Devil. Christ 'descended into Hell' and his suffering was the ransom price that purchased our whole salvation.

Early in the second millennium Anslem, the Archbishop of Canterbury, argued that this gave the Devil too much power. Who, then, could be the ransomer of souls? Only one other candidate in town was qualified to take the post.

Christ's death, Anslem reasoned, 'satisfied' a God whose feudal honour human sin had offended. Later, John Calvin sharpened this up into the penal substitution theory of the Atonement. God was 'armed for vengeance', but out of love for the Elect, and they alone, sent Christ to take their punishment.

The problem with such blood atonement is its seeming sanction of redemptive violence. A God armed for vengeance nods too readily towards the blasphemous idolatry of HMS Vengeance here at Faslane; and that, beneath a sovereign Commander in Chief, who doubles as Defender of the Faith.

What then, for this third millennium, might be the meaning of the Cross? Who, or what, this ransomer of souls? Whither a liberation theory of 'atonement'?

I came today from Govan further up the Clyde; many of my neighbours ransomed unto violence through its face of poverty. That draws me to a single paragraph in a book, *Mon Dieu, Pourquoi?*, where the late Abbé Pierre, a radical French priest, wrote of his wrestling with the ransom question. Was it the Devil, or God? he'd asked. Then came his breakthrough:

'The drug addict,' he wrote, *'... is at the same time his own executioner and the victim. He is both the ransomer and the hostage ... It is the same with all human beings. Because we are disconnected from our authentic divine source, we have become our own executioners. We are slaves to our disordered desires, to our egotism.'*

The Cross, the supreme transformative symbol of non-violence, absorbs in its forgiveness all chains that bind us. Here is the love that dies for love, yet being of eternity, never dies. And so, 'we call this Friday good'.

Christ said: 'I come to bring fire to the earth, and wish it were already kindled!' (Luke 12:49). Let us listen with our healing ear. What kind of fire?

The fire of Hell, of Trident's holocaust? Or the fire of love. That is why we witness at Faslane. That is why we bite the bullet, so unfashionably; why we today survey the wondrous Cross.

Alastair McIntosh

A PEACEFUL LAND

What is being a nation? A talent springing in the heart. And
love of country? Keeping house among a cloud of witnesses.

– Waldo Williams

When one hundred thousand people
met to march from Glasgow Green,
there were millions more walked with them,
a cloud of witnesses unseen,
from the past and from the future,
and the cry on every hand,
'Not in our name do you go to war,
this must be a peaceful land.'

And how shall we teach our children
love of country, pride of place?
Shall we say, we once were heroes
of a fiery, fighting race;
and forget the stains of violence –
people beaten, enslaved and banned?
Or shall we now be peacemakers
in a hospitable land?

From the Pentland to the Solway,
from the Forth down to the Clyde,
city streets and quiet places
and the turning of the tide;

shall we rise on wings of eagles
soaring over wave and sand,
never seeing beneath the surface
to the scars upon the land?

We are armoured and defended
like an empire dressed for war.
But we face no threat or peril
and we don't know what it's for.
'Take the missiles from the waters',
it's our dream and our demand.
Turn the weapons into ploughshares,
give us back a peaceful land.

There's a choice that lies before us.
How shall Scotland best be known?
For the glories of its history
and its loveliness alone?
Or shall care for all earth's people
be the song for which we stand,
and the flowering of our nation
as a just and peaceful land?

Kathy Galloway

AROUND THE WORLD

FORGIVENESS

In late September 1957 nine African-American teenagers exercised their right to attend the previously all white high school in Little Rock, Arkansas. Although protected by the National Guard sent by President Eisenhower the 'Little Rock Nine,' as they were later known, were subjected to abuse, violence and humiliation from many of their white fellow students. The world's press showed several of their faces twisted in a pose of hatred. One of the 'Nine' was Professor Terence Roberts, who founded a Centre for Justice and Reconciliation in California. Some years ago he received a telephone call from one of the white students who had yelled abuse at him and his colleagues nearly fifty years previously. He promised to meet her when he was next in Little Rock. She told him that her life for half a century had been blighted by that incident and she asked for his forgiveness. He graciously helped her to find release. Hearing that story from Terry Roberts in this century reminded me of Martin Luther King's dictum that segregation was a system that imprisoned those who promoted it as well as those who suffered its evil effects.

Iain Whyte

THE ARCHBISHOP CHAIRS THE FIRST SESSION

The Truth and Reconciliation Commission.
April 1996. East London, South Africa

On the first day
after a few hours of testimony
the Archbishop wept.
He put his grey head
on the long table
of papers and protocols
and he wept.

The national
and international cameramen
filmed his weeping,
his misted glasses,
his sobbing shoulders,
the call for a recess.

It doesn't matter what you thought
of the Archbishop before or after,
of the settlement, the commission,
or what the anthropologists flying in
from less studied crimes and sorrows
said about the discourse,
or how many doctorates,
books and installations followed,
or even if you think this poem
simplifies, lionises
romanticises, mystifies.

There was a long table, starched purple vestment
and after a few hours of testimony,
the Archbishop, chair of the commission,
laid down his head, and wept.

That's how it began.

Ingrid de Kok

THE TROUBLES: POEMS FROM THE TRIDEUM

The day God called
through the flames
after the blast
the sheep were safely scattered
as was glass and air
that sucked back, blowing
instant death, insistent
through the doorways.

'Set my people free' called God
from the growing flames
to empty ears and sirens.
'My people long in anguish live –
set my people free;

their warnings late and mine still later –
set my people free.'

God called till night and rain
extinguished what the firemen could not reach
and we would see in mortuaries and wards –
the holy ground once more.

Maundy Thursday

For twenty years that nameless death
– the details grinding the soul –
hung in silent memory.

All night he hung
nicked with knives
in the empty mill,
wrung back to consciousness
when mercy intervened.

Towards dawn
a woman waking on the other side
heard the shriek –
Eloi. Kill me.

They found the body
the throat cut
beside the dustbins
wet with rain.
Someone counted the wounds –

over two hundred.
It was part of the job.

For twenty years that nameless night
crossed with our fear.

One day the new neighbour told
of the mild bachelor
who mended the widow's latch
and wandered homewards
taking a pint in a safe bar.
His last Eucharist.

'They killed my two uncles.
Tim they shot. Frank, that was worse.'

Christ, hanging in a tilting world,
was your pain briefer?
Or was the mill your olive-press that night?

In memory of a victim of sectarian abduction

Good Friday morning

Where sand-dunes bloom and the spring wind blows
and the grey goose comes to rest;
by hardened hearths in the blackened north
the sparrow finds room for her nest;
where the widowed Christ blesses children's eyes
when drawn away to her death,

where God walks slow through the barren lands
with broken hands bearing wedding bands,
and speaks to the lives gone young;

where whispered words count the cost of the curse
that lies on the acid heath,
where worn fields yield through denial and greed
the courtesy of God;
with food for hands that were washed and wrung,
with wine for the bloodied palms,
where bullets shriek through the poisoned streets,
where the gutters choke with lies;
with eyes to the hills and the cost of the kill
the bittern drinks his fill.

At the gap in the hedge by the ruined bridge
where Christ sat down to a meal,
in the burnt-out bones of darkened homes
and the still of a winter field;
at the sharp retort of the sudden crowd
and stones on the metal van
as it moves from the court to the beating place,
where cries resound through the city's wound,
where Christ was alone with the price of his grace
the swallow nests her brood.

Where he called for his mum at the point of the gun
and the stars rose clear and sure,
where courage high carried over the bar
the box that ticked his hour,

where the friend helped out and the braking screeched,
at the package, bomb and steel;
in the battering blows to the hijacked foe,
with clothing ripped and the city stripped,
with the scatter of brains and the shattering gains,
where the blast mixed blood and rain;

where Christ was killed on the whin-gold hills
where the sounds and the eagles wheel,
where God died at the side of the border road
that winds through divided souls;
with arms laid wide on the Narrows' tide,
with empty eyes and an open side;

where the grey wing spreads and the small birds rest
and the foxes find their hole,
where peace from the grief lies beyond our belief,
where the aching years give no fill of relief
only broken hands may reach.

Good Friday evening, Belfast Covenant, 1988

That dark Good Friday with the heavy air
beating our anger as the gutters poured,
soaking the poisoned streets, the extra mile
torn to harm, our arms scarred
vision stained, souls drained,
our feet leaked blood that streamed,
streamed on the pavements
with no hope spared;

that afternoon
with faith subdued,
price paid, spirit dulled
in the trickling lull
of dank chapels
dripping psalms,

we came, under iron cloud,
lifting eyes to the hills

where, sudden, full, unbidden,
three rainbows showed,
grew, glowed, bowed
over the city waste.

Lent 1988 was a particularly violent time, and all parties were implicated.

Holy Saturday

It may be God
has asked the dead
to paint the skies
the colours of their lives.

A limpid blue
by every child
who never smiled
or stayed the briefest while.

The listless pale
when trees are bare

by those whose way
was faded, inward care.

The sea-grey rain
by those who tried
keep courage high
to crest, and sometimes failed.

Pale golden rays
beneath steel grey
for those whose days
were loneliness and pain.

The sunset's shine
by those who prized
their gift, whose music guides
the way we take.

A stormy morning's
blood-tinged clouds
by those whose dread
had left their lives confused.

The silent dawn
that melts the day
by those who pray
and in their stillness light our way.

The golden burst
by those lives stained
by ancient curse
that makes love hard to trust.

The clearest green
of sunset rays
by those who gave
the bravery we praise.

And fading grey
as pearl by those who
saved and served
until the strength was gone.

It may be God
has asked the dead
to paint the skies
the colours of their lives.

And then God left the dark,
that stars that shine on grief and joy and hope
might blossom in a night no clouds conceal.

Easter Sunday morning

After the ceasefire
Jesus cooked a meal.
The Lord Chief Justice came
curious, his wife with trepidation.
The fox strutted out of his hole,
brushed, sleek,
and found his desires before him:
Joanna took him in hand.
The son of the father was washed,
slicked, shocked and supported

by Martha and Matthew, and met his replacement.
There was a hush when Judas pushed
the gate and Magdalen moved up.
Simon arrived from manoeuvres,
dirty red hands carried rounds,
sisters paid prices, bought spices,
there were children grown bent who went straight
when the doors of the shore were opened
and the wounded came in and sat down.

Bless us all

Bless us all.
Forgive us all:
the thieves and the Samaritans;
those that fall by the wayside
and the priests who pass by without stopping;
all our neighbours,
the villains and the victims,
the cursing and the cursed,
those who rebel against you
and those who abandon themselves to your love.
Take us all
into you,
holy and just God.

From the Russian Orthodox liturgy, translated from French

Rosemary Power

THE LAND OF UNLIKENESS:
CHURCHES AND RECONCILIATION

Christian faith challenges all exclusive claims of tribe, tradition and political commitment. The gospel invites us into the space created by Christ and to find there those who were previously our enemies. It therefore seeks to break down the enmity between us: enmity caused by different traditions, and national, political and religious loyalties. The gospel opens up for us a view of wholeness, justice and living in right relations which sees the whole world as potential brothers and sisters; a nourishing and fulfilment of the human. This is a vision of a new humanity reconciled in Christ and living together in a new community.

Through Christ a new relationship is established between those who accept the gift of reconciliation: strangers become citizens and aliens are recognised as members of the household of God (Eph 2:19). This redeemed people are called to be a community of reconciliation – a community of openness and inclusion – united round the death and resurrection of Jesus Christ.

At the same time, the reality is that churches are part of communities and nations; they cannot be other. They are chaplains, reflectors, consciences, restrainers, discerners, givers of wisdom, custodians of collective memory and places of community belonging. Churches bring 'their' community before God. They are places where the 'specialness' and stories of communities and nations can be celebrated. Much of this is necessary and good, but there is another side. 'Specialness' can lead to exclusivity and a sense of superiority. Churches can be places where we are told – implicitly and explicitly – who does not belong to our community: by who is prayed for and who is not, by the contents of sermons, and by the symbols displayed or not displayed.

The church is a home for the community or the nation. And at the same time it lives by a story of a Jesus who died outside the camp (Heb 13:13) and who, while completely a Jew, did not belong to his world (Jn 17:14) and was driven out of it by those who did not want to be disturbed by another way. All our 'homes' – personal, communal, national – are radically de-centred by Jesus: *'For there is no eternal city for us in this life, but we look for one in the life to come'* (Heb 13:14). And the church is a community where Jew and Greek and free belong (1 Cor 12:13); in its very essence it transcends all social, cultural and national boundaries.

The church lives in a tension: in the world, but not of it (cf. Jn 18:36). The danger is that in situations of communal conflict the tension collapses and, as the Croatian theologian Miroslav Volf says: ... Churches often find themselves accomplices in war rather than agents of peace. We find it difficult to distance ourselves from our own culture so we echo its reigning opinions and mimic its practices.[1]

The Janus face of religion

Religion plays a profoundly ambiguous role in conflict situations. On the one hand, it can encourage hatred; anti-Catholicism is particularly potent in Northern Ireland, and has political consequences. Churches can reinforce community division and harden boundaries; Catholic views and rules on mixed marriage and the importance of church schools have had significant consequences in Northern Irish society. Religion can give divine sanction to nationalisms, political positions and violence. Shimon Peres says of Hezbollah, the Lebanese Shiite terrorist group: *'These are religious people. With the religious you can hardly negotiate. They think they have supreme permission to kill people and go to war. This is their nature'.*[2] In conflict situations theologies of enmity, superiority and distorted recognition of others can easily gain prominence, e.g. the Dutch Reformed Church in South Africa theologically legitimated apartheid. When churches and religions find themselves on different sides of a fear-threat relationship between two communities, there can be a political/religious symbiosis, e.g. in Northern Ireland – Protestantism/Unionism, Catholicism/Nationalism.

Churches find it difficult to establish any critical distance from the pressures coming from 'their' community. The temptation is to identify without reserve and to become chaplains to 'their' community. Ian Linden has written about the *'stranglehold that ethnicity had gained'* in the church in Rwanda. The church *'had never seriously challenged Hutu or Tutsi identity as potentially open to being re-imagined in a Christian form, because ethnicity had always been taken as a given'.*[3] When the genocide occurred in 1994 the church found it very difficult to resist the dynamics of hatred and killing. There were a significant number of prominent Christians involved in the killings (although there were church people who resisted and were martyred).

On the other hand, religion can be a force for restraint and this has been generally true in Northern Ireland. Without the churches the situation would have been a lot worse; the preaching and living out of non-retaliation, forbearance and forgiveness has had real social consequences. The churches opposed those who espoused violence and the gods of nationalism. Churches working together have been a force for good; they have helped lessen the religious/political symbiosis. And, nevertheless, the picture is very mixed and deeply ambiguous. Some black, much grey, a little white. Churches are part of the problem, and struggle to be part of the solution.

The church in Fiji illustrates this well. During the coup in 1987 by the military (many of the instigators were deeply steeped in Christian practice and openly invoked their faith as a guide for their action) the temptation was strong to align the church to the interests of chauvinist politicians who seized control of the state and sought legitimation of their rule that pitched one ethnic community against another. It fell upon another set of church leaders to defy the military and secular authorities in advocating an alternative course of reconciliation.[4]

The problem is that politics appears to dominate the churches more than vice versa. This is one very significant factor in inhibiting churches in being agents of cooperation and raises profound questions about what is more important: religious commitment or political commitment. In theological terms, we are talking about the issue of idolatry.

Churches tend to reflect people's fears, reflect community divisions, reflect a community experience of violence and threat, rather than act as agents of change or transformers of conflict. Thus the Protestant Churches in Northern Ireland often talked about law and order, reflecting a community under siege, and the Catholic Church often talked about justice, reflecting a community feeling of victimisation. Churches not only reflect people's fears; they can also amplify them (witness the role of the Rev Dr Ian Paisley in Northern Ireland until recently).

In divided societies, fear, anxiety and a sense of threat are encoded; they almost become part of people's genetic make-up. As the dynamics of conflict gather force, individuals and groups disappear into a vortex of antagonism. They are magnetised by violence. It takes very strong people to stand out when all around succumb. And it is true that some people can stand outside the vortex of antagonism.

In Northern Ireland some church people are the most committed in terms of peace and reconciliation, common witness and cooperation and have been so since the start of the 'Troubles'. In Rwanda, some Christians were martyred for standing against the ethnic hatred and killing. In Fiji some Christian leaders resisted the coup and stood for reconciliation between ethnic groups.

Transcendent faith

The church is a witness to the Kingdom of God and the presence of transcendence, and is called to be a community of reconciliation and as such offer a 'space' in the world for those who believe that human society can, if only in anticipation, overcome its violent origins, its continuing resentments and mistrust and come to realise its true calling to become the beloved community envisaged by the biblical story.[5]

Thus the church exists that we may know what humanity might be, that is, people who are 'different' and 'strange':

- able to stand out against community hatred;
- able to cross community boundaries;
- able to be peacemakers;
- able to be healers;
- able to forgive;
- able to stand with the victims;
- able to engage in costly action.

When we see this 'difference' and 'strangeness' we are in the presence of transcendence and in the presence of witness to the Kingdom of God. The message of reconciliation is made visible.

I am a member of a community of reconciliation, the Corrymeela Community. Corrymeela has worked, often residentially, with a huge mixture of people from all sorts of different backgrounds. We have been journeying together for over forty years and there are 'graduates' of Corrymeela all over the place. During that time we have learnt the importance of:

- belonging together in a community of diversity;
- reconciliation being a practice, and a journey, not a theory or a strategy or a technique;
- a safe space where people can come and meet each other, where there is an atmosphere of trust and acceptance and where differences can be acknowledged, explored and accepted;
- presence and accompaniment – people who can give time and attention;
- a community of faith being able to bring healing, and so being a 'touching place';
- encounter and relationships; it is only in encounter and relationships that words like trust, reconciliation and forgiveness become real;
- acknowledging and sharing vulnerability;
- people telling their stories and listening to other people's stories. Our identities and lives are based strongly on the stories we tell about ourselves, our families, our communities, our countries. Thus we need places where memories are explored and untangled;
- not writing people off as incorrigible 'baddies' no matter what they

have done – this is not to trivialise evil or say wrong does not matter;

- the avoidance of self-righteousness and an awareness of our own hypocrisy;
- surprise and the unexpected; reconciliation is something given as well as a practice;
- taking small steps;
- being sustained and nourished by hope and a vision of a different future;
- being involved for the long haul; and
- a recognition that the transformation of the world is linked to the transformation of ourselves.

David Stevens, 2004

NOTES:
1. Miroslav Volf, 'A Vision of Embrace', *Ecumenical Review,* April, 1995
2. *The New Yorker,* October 14 and 21, 2002
3. Ian Linden, 'The Churches and Genocide: Lessons from the Rwandan Genocide' in *The Reconciliation of Peoples: Challenge to the Churches*, Gregory Baum and Harold Wells (Eds), World Council of Churches Publications, 1997, p.52
4. Ralph R Premdas 'The Church and Reconciliation in Ethnic Conflicts: The Case of Fiji' in Baum and Wells (Eds), op.cit., p.93
5. Lewis Mudge, source unknown

SEA-GLASS

*This poem was written for a team of Community Dialogue
facilitators from Scotland visiting the Corrymeela Community
in Northern Ireland. The image of glass here was first inspired
by Duncan Morrow, the Scottish Government's Advisor on
sectarianism, who at Corrymeela spoke about glass ceilings
and glass bottles in our response to sectarianism. Katrina
Crosby first introduced me to the wonders of sea-glass on Iona.*

It's rubbish, really, this sea-glass:
this brown, blue, green glass
tossed round and round;
smoothed – cloudy, clear –
by the surf
and the slow swift tides
that wash between us.

So when did it turn into a weapon?
A sharpened shard
hurled to hurt, to kill
the space and the peace between us.
Or a prison?
This glass ceiling,
this level beyond which I cannot move,
by which I am boxed, defined, confined,
excluded and exiled,
has fenced us out.
And then a glass curtain?
Toxic, really toxic too,

the sometimes civil
screeching of our suspicions
across invisible barricades and
through naked walls built in the night
and in the name of 'keeping the peace'.

Where a broken mosaic is offered
as space for courageous conversation
perhaps there
is a place for hope.

Ruth Harvey
Head of Training and Peacebuilding
Place for Hope

AFGHANISTAN, 1997

Twenty years ago I lived in Afghanistan, working for a charity. This was a time of civil war, before September 11th and the subsequent NATO invasion. These pieces draw on some of my experiences at the time and thoughts since. In war, the normal structure of society is jettisoned; there is violence, terror and God can seem absent. 'The patch' uses the image of mine-clearance workers, who need to check the ground inch by inch. War means that their work, and the work of reconciliation, must begin again.

– Tim Aldred

Evacuated

When the bomb fell
from an antique MIG –
more to teach a lesson
than a serious attempt to retake the town –
there was a sound before
which cut over the calls of shopkeepers
and the silence of spring-blue sky:
a machine swooping.

Drop to the floor and lie there,
feeling foolish for a second; maybe two seconds,
until the crack
and the window shattering upstairs.

That's not good, says my housemate.
I lift my eyes to see the pillar of cloud:
our house was in the pilot's sights this time.

The safest thing, to stay behind the gate, discreet
away from the tired eyes of fighters.
Wait. Dig in. Sit it out.
But privacy feeds the fear.
What gives comfort is to go and look:
see how the shrapnel falls across the valley,
see them prepare the launcher,
scan the sky;
at least you see it coming.

The radio: we should go.
I look at my room, my carefully gathered things,
_____ unk, leave it.

*War on
the Poor*   ee :he press that night
          y   ad the other way
          ,   tory.

        I re urn.
     ur while with a neighbour
        ter had died.
        ink it helps.

     ver *not afraid,* my colleague said.
     _ . t *right, I was afraid,* I said, embarrassed.
        e replied, *I know.*

The fight

What was strange about the fight
was that although
like ants scenting intruders
they were readying to dismember each other in the passages,
the wind still blew gently across a blue sky.
As I ran to find shelter I bought a loaf of bread
and one of the soldiers asked me to stop and drink tea.

The patch

We fancied ourselves clearing away stones,
on our knees
in the sights of an old enemy,
freeing a patch from the weight of old armour
left behind from our last rule.
A patch which could become a garden.
The honourable span their dice
believing themselves surgeons,
finding themselves butchers.
People like us moved to kill again
and scatter new mines.
Futile to protest this was not of our making.

A few approach on their knees still
back towards the patch.
Inch by inch.

Tim Aldred

PRAYER FOR AFGHANISTAN

Lord, you have never left Afghanistan.
You made its fields, mountains and streams.
You made all of its people in your image.
You have been present throughout its history.

We confess that we have been at war in Afghanistan,
that this war has caused terrible suffering and death
and has deepened hatred between people.
We confess that we have so far failed to bring peace.

We pray for all the people of Afghanistan.
We pray for those on all sides who have fought, and who still fight.
We pray especially for those who now grieve,
and for those who have suffered physical or mental injury.

Teach us all how to bring peace, friendship and healing.
Comfort, strengthen and inspire the people of Afghanistan
as they work to build a better future.
And give courage, wisdom and humility to all who work alongside them.

Amen

Tim Aldred

BOUNDARIES

A reflection on serving as a peace monitor with the Ecumenical Accompaniment Programme in Palestine and Israel (EAPPI)

The tiny village of Yanoun is only mentioned in the Bible once. In the book of Joshua there's a very long account of how territory was divided up among the tribes of Israel. Chapter 16:5,6 describes *'the boundary of the Ephraimites family by family … going round by the east of Taanath-shiloh and passing by it on the east of Janoah'*. Janoah/Yanoun then was just a marker in the making of boundaries. Yanoun today is a small farming community, where boundaries have positive and negative meanings.

I talked to Rashed, the mayor and one of the farmers who work the valley which runs between Upper Yanoun, at its head, and Lower Yanoun, where the land opens out. As well as a flock of sheep and goats, he has olive groves and fields under plough. We were looking out over the valley bottom, a patchwork of green – with hay, chickpeas, broad beans and wheat. 'You don't build walls or put up fences,' I said. 'Then how do you know where your land begins and ends?' He laughed, 'It is my land – I plough it and plant it. Kemal's land is right next door. If he want, he can put a stone at each corner. But if he don't put a stone, I know. Each year I plough the land. I know where the rocks are, underneath the soil.'

He knows the land well. This is where his father and grandfather farmed before him. But the landscape has changed. The tops of the limestone hills, which were once open grazing land stretching all the way down to the Jordan Valley, now bustle with watchtowers, telecommunication towers, water-towers, caravans, polytunnels and big chicken barns. These are the illegal outposts of the settlement of Itamar.

Rashed says that the traditional lands of Upper and Lower Yanoun amounted to 16,500 *dunums*. But now only at most 500 *dunums* are actually accessible to Upper Yanoun. 'Lower Yanoun is better. Here, we are in the middle of settlements.' He gestured round the hilltops, wearily.

There is limited access to another 400 *dunums*. The previous week he was able to get a one-day permit from the DCO to plough some of his own land, which is high on the hill near the settlement. But the next day, when he went back to graze his goats nearby, he was chased away by masked men. Soldiers or settlers? It wasn't clear. What was clear was that he had overstepped the mark.

Who sets the mark? 'Who decides where the boundaries will be?' I asked.

'The soldiers and settlers together decide. When the settlers want to change it, the soldiers agree.'

How are the boundaries marked? 'On this side' (to the west of the village) 'they make a fence.' It is visible on the skyline – not a huge structure like the Separation Barrier, just the way anyone might define their property. But whose property? These outposts are illegal in Israeli as well as international law. The young men who have come out from Itamar to stake a claim here are squatters on the land of Rashed and his neighbours. But now that this settlement expansion is becoming a 'fact on the ground', maybe it's good to have the ground marked out – don't 'good fences make good neighbours'? It's not as simple as that: 'There they made a fence – we can see the fence. But we can't go near it. If we even go so far,' he indicates several hundred metres, 'they will come out and give us trouble.'

I was struggling to understand what was going on, when I read this 'idiot's guide' from the organisation that brings together former Israeli soldiers and Palestinian fighters, Combatants for Peace:

> *So this is how it works: The settlers arrive at a certain hill and construct an outpost, which is actually a caravan or a wooden shelter. This hill is usually privately owned Palestinian land. The army and the state give legitimacy to these actions by the fact that when these outposts are constructed the soldiers arrive straight away and guard it, of course, protecting the settlers. The owners of the land cannot harvest it any more. The party isn't over yet: around a settlement a special security zone is announced; the Palestinians aren't allowed to enter. Its size and area, no one really knows. The Palestinians find this out through trial and error: if they get caught and beaten they know they reached this zone. Of course there isn't any official decision, and when the units of soldiers change, so do their ground rules. And so the game starts over.* (*Combatants for Peace Newsletter*, July 2009).

The invisible boundaries encroach on the village. And they are constantly being redefined. For instance, barns for battery chickens or other huge agricultural buildings, such as those above Yanoun, not only attract subsidy from the Israeli Government, but also carry with their large footprint the need for a bigger 'security zone' – which effectively enlarges the settlement area. As we talk, we watch several Palestinian shepherds grazing their flocks along the roadside or in the olive groves – while the hillsides lie inviting and empty, they are no-go areas for the farmers. Meanwhile the settlers sometimes choose to stroll through this landscape with impunity – almost as though they are 'beating the bounds' – defining their territory.

Here is Rashed's story of a recent incident – an attack not with weapons but with humiliating words: 'I go with my sheep ... maybe 200 metres beyond the house. One settler came ... he approached me with an M16. I saw there were two more settlers on the hill. He asked me what I am doing here. I say "Feeding my sheep." He says, "No, this land is for me. Go to your home."

'I say, "You ask me to leave this place. Where shall I go? When I go to another place another person ask me to leave. So where shall I go?" He says, "You want to make problems here? You need problems here? No! Go to your home!" What to do? Perhaps they shoot my sheep ... I leave with my sheep.'

All the time we are talking, a bulldozer is working on the hilltop to the east, breaking new ground. Rashed points out that it's not a contractor, but an army bulldozer: 'Not settlers, army. That is bad.' Whatever military structure is planned there, this activity identifies the army of occupation more closely with the planting of settlements. The appropriate boundaries in their relationship were crossed and abandoned some time ago.

Rashed makes this connection, remembering a time before 1993, when Itamar was founded. He was 15 years old and was with his father and their flocks upon the hill where the chicken barns now stand. 'Soldiers come and start shooting over our heads. That was before the settlers. We go back to our house.' It was as though that was an early sign of the boundaries being redefined by force. Since then, when first the settlement and then the outposts came, Yanoun has suffered, but survived the crisis in 2002, when its people fled escalating violence. It's now the eighth year of international presence here – embodied most of the time by EAPPI – which seems to limit the aggression of the settlers and the military. But there's little we can do to hold back the invisible boundaries which are tightening like a noose on this valley.

'You know the settlers, the Israelis, want to take over the whole land – want to take Palestinian people outside the whole land. But if soldiers want to take me, and my wife and children outside our home, if they want to shoot us, I not go. Where will I go?'

Jan Sutch Pickard

FATHER FRANS OF HOMS (1938-2014)

He refused to leave.
He knew his place.
It was his home.

He refused security.
He knew his task.
They were his people.

He refused safety.
He knew his God.
They were his people.

Jesuit Father Frans van der Lugt had lived in Syria for nearly fifty years and refused safe passage out of the city of Homs. A brief cessation of conflict at the beginning of the year had meant that there was an opportunity for him to leave with the young and wounded but he refused.

He stayed in his monastery to serve the small number of Christians still in the city. He explained his rejection of evacuation in these terms:

'I don't see people as Muslims or Christians. I see a human being first and foremost. I am the shepherd of my flock.'

We tried our best.
We made it easy.
But he would not come.

His flock had scattered.
They were hardly there.
But he would not leave.
The Call had not been withdrawn.
There is a greater love.
His Lord was the Way.

Father Frans now joins a path given to a long line of Christians who have refused to leave. The intransigent servant of the will of God is an important figure in the story of Christian devotion. They remind us that at the heart of calling there is humility and obedience. They arrive at a moment in their life when to refuse common sense is the more important thing to do. They resist the advice of those who are deemed to know better. It is the time of the emptying of self, as did their Lord.

They do not court admiration. They do not seek to be an example. They carry a cross and live with the consequences.

He spoke our language.
He lived our way.
We were one.

He looked deep.
He became our flesh.
We were made whole.

He lived by grace.
He died for peace.
His blood was shed.

Friend, of whom do you speak?

John Rackley

PRAYING WITH THE EARTH

Is there anything more important to do than pray for peace, and in particular pray for peace within the family of Abraham and Sarah and Hagar? The shadow side of Christianity, Judaism and Islam is at the heart of some of the most conflicted places of hatred and violence in our world today. We know the frightened and angry countenance of religion. We need to look it in the face and denounce it as a false expression. But do we also know that deep within our religious inheritance are visions and practices of peacemaking that hold the key to transformation in our lives and world? We desperately need to access these now. Without peace in the family of Abraham there will not be peace among us as nations.

Praying with the Earth, along with its companion CD of meditative chants, *Chanting for Peace*, is a peace-offering from within the Christian household. In this prayer book and collection of chants, sentences from the Quran, the Hebrew Scriptures and the teachings of Jesus are used in order to pray for peace, allowing words from other parts of the family to draw us back to the true roots of our inheritance, the oneness of the human soul and the essential unity of the earth.

The inspiration for this project grew out of my teaching relationship in the high desert of New Mexico with Nahum Ward-Lev and Rahmah Lutz, a Rabbi from Santa Fe and a Sufi Muslim teacher from Abiquiu. Every summer my wife Ali and I co-teach with Nahum and Rahmah on themes of peace within the Abrahamic community. Our daily pattern is to take it in turn. Whichever one of us is teaching offers words of scripture from our respective tradition for the group to take into silence before shared reflection and conversation.

The first summer together I offered our class words from St Matthew's Gospel. As people meditatively walked in the desert landscape or sat prayerfully in the coolness of the adobe chapel, I noticed that Rahmah's face was radiant. Her countenance always shines but on this occasion she looked like Moses coming down from Mount Sinai. I wondered what was happening in her heart. When we gathered, she was the first to speak. She said, 'I so love Jesus, peace be upon him. He is so compassionate. He is so truthful. He is so merciful. I so love Jesus, peace be upon him.' Most of us in the circle were from the Christian household. And many of us sat with tears in our eyes. As I looked at Rahmah I thought: *You are teaching us how to speak about Jesus.*

If Jesus' wisdom is again to be recovered within the Christian household, in ways that will enable us to lead the world in peace rather than divide the world in hatred, I believe its rebirth will come largely from outside Christianity. Other parts of the Abrahamic family have not forgotten the essence of Jesus – his compassion, his truthfulness, his mercy. It is from them that we will be helped to remember the true heart of Jesus. And it is from them that we will be helped to remember how to truly follow Jesus.

We need one another. Our traditions are given not to compete with each other. They are given to complete each other. This is my hope in *Praying with the Earth*. This is my intention in *Chanting for Peace*. In listening to the true heart of Islam and Judaism, we will be led not away from the true heart of Christianity; we will be led to a recovery of our distinct treasure, the wisdom of Jesus, who taught us to pray for peace, and who showed us how to live love.

These new resources are only two particular expressions of the way forward. It is of course not just a prayer book and a collection of meditative chants that we need. Our deep need and our truest desire is for greater relationship within the Abrahamic family. Relationship, relationship, relationship is what will change us as individuals and as traditions. And it is the re-establishing of relationship that will heal us. The Praying for Peace Initiative, which I and others launched at the beginning of 2011, is committed to praying and chanting for peace by using the words and wisdom of other parts of the family. It is a way of becoming more deeply aware of one another's treasure. Many members of the Christian household have never read the Quran, let alone used its words to pray. Shall we choose in new ways to live in relationship?

People often think that peace is a pipe dream. In part this is because the word 'peace' has been limitedly associated with a future kingdom or a perfect realm of God on earth. And so the impression has been created that if true peace were to come it would be forever, as if eternally established. But is this the nature of relationship? Who are the people who are most important to us in our lives? They are the people who have chosen again and again and again to look to our heart and to remain in relationship with us even when we have been false. And the reverse is also true about the most important relationships of life. In every moment of our lives and world we have the capacity to choose to be untrue, whether as individuals, as nations, or as a species. This is the challenge, as well as the beauty, of life in its interwovenness. True relationship must always be chosen. This is its greatest blessing. I can look to your heart and honour you now, or I can look away from your heart and dishonour you now. And so the way of peace is not about thinking that we need to create a perfect realm of relationship that will hold forever. It is about choosing to be true to one another in every moment, again and again and again. The time of peace is now. Now is the time to make our offering.

To the home of peace
to the field of love
to the land where forgiveness and right relationship meet
we look, O God,
with longing for earth's children
with compassion for the creatures
with hearts breaking for the people and nations we love.
Open us to visions we have never known
strengthen us for self-givings we have never made
delight us with a oneness we could never have imagined
that we may truly be born of You
makers of peace.

- from *Praying with the Earth*[1]

John Philip Newell

NOTE:

1. *Praying with the Earth: A prayer book for peace*, John Philip Newell, SCM/Canterbury Press, 2010. Used by permission of John Philip Newell.

I ASKED ...

Ten years ago I was working as a volunteer teacher-trainer in Kashmir. I read the following short prayer on the staffroom noticeboard and copied it down. Over the years I have often reflected on these words, and have found them to be a great source of strength ...

I asked for strength
and Allah gave me difficulties to make me strong.

I asked for wisdom
and Allah gave me problems to solve.

I asked for prosperity
and Allah gave me brain and brawn to work.

I asked for courage
and Allah gave me dangers to overcome.

I asked for love
and Allah gave me troubled people to help.

I asked for favours
and Allah gave me opportunities.

I received nothing I wanted.
I received everything I needed.

Source unknown, from Catherine Oxworth

REFLECTION FROM IONA ABBEY

Services on a Monday evening here in the Abbey focus on issues of justice, peace and the integrity of creation. When I started thinking about this particular Monday evening service, which is partly a service of welcome for our guests, the first thing that came to my mind was the phrase 'Peace be with you'. In biblical times, it was a common greeting, and Jesus himself is quoted as saying it on various occasions. In fact, even today in Arabic- and Hebrew-speaking cultures folk greet each other with '*Shalom aleichem*' and '*As-salamu alaykum*', which translate into 'Peace be with you', and are the equivalent of our 'Hi!'.

In our culture, most people, myself included, would probably look a bit startled being addressed with 'Peace be with you', but I do like the idea of wishing everybody I encounter *peace*, and having that same wish repeated to me. Maybe if all of us took that notion to heart, together we could build the foundations of a more just and peaceable society.

I invite you now to greet someone you haven't spoken with before: greet them with a sign of peace, and then share with them what working for peace means to you …

> Peace on each one who comes in need,
> PEACE ON EACH ONE WHO COMES IN JOY.
> Peace on each one who offers prayers,
> PEACE ON EACH ONE WHO OFFERS SONG.
> Peace of the Maker, Peace of the Son,
> PEACE OF THE SPIRIT, THE TRIUNE ONE.
> (*A prayer from Iona Abbey*)

Dagmar Erdmann

THE NONVIOLENT PEACEFORCE MEET THE ARROW BOYS

From our base in Nzara we travelled by Land Cruiser for two hours through the lush green forest on red rutted roads, splashing through puddles up to our door panels. We stopped in a *boma* (village) a few kilometres from the border with the Democratic Republic of the Congo (DRC). We were in the heart of what is referred to as the 'LRA-affected areas': those parts of South Sudan, the DRC and the Central Africa Republic where Joseph Kony and the Lord's Resistance Army operate.

It was the rainy season. Crops would be harvested soon – and the LRA would be coming to look for food.

We met with 25 'Arrow Boys' and the chief of the *payam*. The Arrow Boys, armed with bows, arrows, spears and homemade single-shot rifles, patrol the bush surrounding their *bomas*. They walk every day through dense undergrowth tolerating rain, mud, tsetse flies and snakes. A few have boots. None have rain gear or first aid supplies.

They are frustrated: when threats appear, it takes the South Sudanese army 2-3 days to respond. UN agencies and NGOs withdraw.

The Arrow Boys see no other way to protect their communities. As one told me: *'It is kill or be taken.'*

So there we were: the Nonviolent Peaceforce and the Arrow Boys.

I admired their courage and commitment. I recalled how Gandhi observed that non-violence and cowardice are contradictory; how he could make a Satyagarahi out of a soldier but that he could not make one from a coward.

We weren't there in a vain attempt to try to convince the Arrow Boys to lay down their weapons. We were there to find our common ground in terms of protecting civilians.

The NP team met the next morning and strategised how to develop a relationship with the Arrow Boys, based on our principles and mandate:

- *Training on conflict: early warning/early response.*
- *Training on unarmed civilian protection, including child protection.*
- *Advocacy with the UN mission to increase their patrols of the area during the harvest season.*
- *A regular presence of NP protectors.*
- *Advocacy on the international level to negotiate a settlement.*

Then we met with the Arrow Boys. It was a humbling encounter.

But the Arrow Boys want to hear back from us. We will return with an offer and talk. NP will remain non-violent. The Arrow Boys will retain their weapons. As we authentically engage with each other, we all will learn a lot.

Mel Duncan, Co-founder Nonviolent Peaceforce

THE SMALL GIRL AND THE BIG MEN: NONVIOLENT PEACEFORCE

'Look at the small girl who came to solve our problems,' recounted a hospital nurse, describing the work of Nonviolent Peaceforce (NP) in Lakes State in South Sudan.

Asha Asokan, from Kerala, is an NP Civilian Protection Officer, who measures barely 5 feet. The Dinka men of Lakes State often tower above 6 feet 5 inches. While small in stature, Asha is a dynamo packed with enthusiasm and experience. She is a lawyer with a Masters degree in Human Rights and International Humanitarian Law. Before coming to NP, she worked for the UN Peacekeeping Mission (UNMIS) in Sudan.

A group of hospital nurses had convened to tell the Nonviolent Peaceforce why NP not only needed to stay in Lakes State, but to increase its presence here. They portrayed a scene where youth from different clans had converged at a cattle camp and were about to break into violence. When NP arrived some were already wounded. NP intervened, with Asha in the lead. They shuttled back and forth between the contending clans.

The youth asked a local NP peacekeeper: '*Who is this small girl, and where does she come from?*' The peacekeeper explained that she had come from India. The youth backed off from each other. 'According to our culture we don't want to do something bad in front of outsiders,' explained one of the nurses. The youth leaders had reasoned: this problem has become so serious that people from other countries are coming. We will stop now.

There was a promise from all sides that they would not fight and that they would wait for the chiefs to come and talk. The next morning the chiefs arrived and mediated a deal. NP monitored the process at the chiefs' request. A violent conflict was averted.

Mel Duncan, Co-founder Nonviolent Peaceforce

NOTE:

These articles were written almost three years ago. Since then so much has changed. South Sudan is embroiled in a vicious war and the economy is on the brink of collapse. We are struggling to keep our 150 people on the ground.

For updated stories on the situation, go to: www.nonviolentpeaceforce.org/news-home. Look at the interview of the two civilian protectors who stood in the door of a hut, protecting 14 women and children, telling the militia that they would not leave.

– Mel Duncan, 2015

MEN ARE THE CAUSE

'To the best of my knowledge, no war was ever started by women.'

– Aung San Suu Kyi, from the Keynote Address at NGO Forum on Women,
Beijing, China, August 31, 1995

Men are the cause
and men are the means.

I see photos of dead mothers
holding their babies;
their blood runs red
in the dirt
on both sides of the border.

There is so much dirt.

A little boy went out to play;
he now lies folded like a rag doll
discarded on the road.
A burst football rolls lazily nearby.

Men are the cause
and men are the means
by which such suffering
is visited upon us.

And there is so much suffering.

In the name of their god
their leader

their book
their tribe
their party
their clan –
in the name of their foul and twisted beliefs
about those who live
on the other side of the line –
men destroy
all that is good in your hearts and mine.

Now is the time for all good men,
aye, and good women too,
to say 'Enough!'

In the name of all those mothers
who lie in the dirt
shielding their babies from hurt,
in the name of all those children
who will never become
what they were meant to become;
in the name of all that is good
on this good earth:
we say 'Enough!'

Men are the cause
and men are the means –
but only good men say
'No more! No more! No more!'

Bryan Owen

WHAT MEN'S HEALING COULD LOOK LIKE, IF WE MEAN IT

As I approach twenty years of managing a therapy service for men who have been sexually traumatised, I ponder the meaning of it all.

Meaning-making – giving a narrative to the unspoken horrors, which can then ultimately be crafted into one's life story – is the ticket for those who are wounded. This is the true 'take-away' from counselling; yet not just meaning-making for the individual involved. In a universal sense, we *all* need to have a necessary conversation about how we define our lives – our pain, our struggles and our need for wholeness.

Recovery usually does not involve healing on the physical plane – but the healing of something that can best be described as soul wounds. The bleeding of the heart. The psychic suffering. The ghosts that do not sleep …

I write this in the midst of a truly international gathering here in Cambodia of advocates committed to eradicating sexual violence against boys and men. Some delegates come from societies where sex is not discussed. Others come from worlds where the only words to suggest sexual offences against men are to describe being 'treated as a woman'. Other folk come from cultures where there is no word for counselling. In some countries, being a male victim of sexual assault, if reported to authorities, could result in the victim's arrest as homosexuality is illegal. The universality of shame is present in all corners of this world – an emotion that demands hiding, not dialogue.

This conference occurs a block away from S-21 – an infamous place of killing during the dark period of history when the Khmer Rouge were in power. A school, now the Tuol Sleng Genocide Museum, was the centre for the murder of up to 20,000 people – men and women, boys and girls.

Babies, too. I saw enough skulls not to question these facts. And here we are, a block or two away from this site, discussing another atrocity in our shared stories of the childhood rape of boys, the adult rape of men, wartime rape, ethnic cleansing rape, clergy rape, prisoner rape. Tuol Sleng is the view from our building when we break for coffee. We talk to each other as if we are unaware of this shadow on the shadow, but we all know.

Despite the darkness, there are many points of light emerging around the world, emerging for the healing of boys and men. People are coming together to speak their truth. Some gatherings look like evangelical meetings where people shout out their stories; some take the appearance of meetings of Alcoholics Anonymous in musty basements; some look like clusters of shipwrecked sailors joining hands in the water as the only means of staying afloat. They almost all take the shape of circles, a thought that seems only right in the making of things whole.

So in this moment of reflection on the courage of so many boys and men in telling their stories, let's take a moment to examine how we can define men's healing:

The *absence of symptoms* is one way we can define men's healing. If we take the dozens of characteristics of post-traumatic stress disorder (PTSD) or of complex PTSD, we could say that healing could be shown by the absence of such symptoms. Like after the surgical removal of a tumour, the healing of a survivor is when his tests come back negative.

The notion of *reconnection* is another option for defining the healing of men. This term is often given to the third and final phase of trauma recovery theory, when the individual can return to the fullness of his or her life no longer needing to self-identify as a victim or survivor. Whether the reconnection is within himself, his family or his community, he can emerge without restriction – free of the confines of his trauma identity.

Testimony – the ability to tell one's whole story, from beginning to end, without omissions, without dissociating and without any 'big' emotions – is another potential framework. Guys in our programme get a session where they can give their testimony to their peers in the circle, which, if completed, is the ticket towards setting their graduation date. Testimony is universal, whether one sees its origins from the 'rap groups' of American soldiers coming back from Vietnam, or victim support in the first rape crisis centres for women.

More and more the term *resiliency* comes up in doing this work. It offers a fuller, more robust expansion of the notion of recovery being the absence of symptoms: not only is the survivor back to a baseline of normality – he is stronger, better, more buoyant in response to life's challenges. Much like the old laundry soap adage of getting your clothes 'whiter than white', resiliency is a value-added notion of healing.

Some survivors of trauma gravitate to the concept of *emotional integrity*: the living of one's life with thoughts, feelings and behaviour being all at one. In particular, there are three separate but intertwined steps to this: 1) being fully honest with oneself, 2) taking responsibility for one's behaviour and feelings and 3) reducing the emotional space between oneself and significant people in one's life. If we consider that many traumas are inflicted due to interpersonal violations (childhood abuse, adult assault, torture and so on) and many aspects of these wounds reappear in relationships, then emotional integrity may fully demonstrate the healing process.

'Walking the sacred path' is an alternative depiction of healing. While we can say that most of us, most of the time, walk through this world on a

'survival path' – working hard to make money, spending money on food and shelter, making the meals and beds and getting the children off to school – then precious few of us spend enough time thinking about why we are on this wondrous planet in the first place. What are our own unique marching orders? What are our true gifts to share with others? If we can not only be aware of this intention, but live it as well, then we are truly on the sacred path.

'Living the good life' is yet another choice for metaphor. The source of this stems from work with offenders. An adjunct of restorative justice, the 'good life' suggests that if we can provide an offender with critical life resources like employment, housing, emotional support and other needs that reflect respect and meaning and compassion, he or she may well not reoffend. Research is showing this approach pays off in spades. Now think if we *all* had the opportunities and the payoffs of the good life, how the quality of life would change and how much farther we could realise belonging, non-violence and love.

Lastly, let's picture for a moment that healing from our wounds could be best described as *boring*. Think about this: imagine that the horror and suffering and all that is attached to the soul murder one has experienced is now so mundane in recall that the process of reflection elicits no big emotions, no big thoughts: it is what it is, and that is all. Isn't that what healing is about? Sure the person can recall what happened (we aren't talking about forgetting – as if that could be possible!), but with the simple ability to recall life's trauma and tell it like one is recapping a movie plot line, or the mundane events of yesterday. While they may prefer not to tell this particular story (the big game may be more fun to discuss, or the new accomplishment of one's child), he or she could talk about it, if they needed to. It just would be boring to them. It would be that simple.

All of these metaphors, I believe, can be useful in working towards a place of healing for men, healing for us all, really. The work involved, of course, ain't easy. But nothing of value in life is.

Rick Goodwin

BUILDING A MODEL CITY
OF PEACE AND HARMONY DOWN UNDER

The history of 'early settlement' in southern Queensland is not happy. Courageous though many European pioneers were, there was great cost. As one leader of the often brutal Native Police infamously reported after one punitive raid upon Aborigines: 'I much regretted not having one hour more daylight as I would have annihilated the lot.' Later came the 'White Australia' Policy, and a continuing tradition of harsh repressive suspicion towards others, embodied in the late-20th-century politicians Joh Bjelke-Petersen and Pauline Hanson. South-east Queensland is therefore in many ways not the most obvious congenial site for reconciliation. Yet appearances can be deceiving.

A few years ago, one of the world's great spiritual teachers, the Venerable Master Chin Kung, had a dream: to build a 'model city' of peace and harmony. He looked around, surveyed many possibilities, and chose … Toowoomba in Queensland! Here he established his Pure Land Learning

College, grew friendship bonds among the local community and nurtured international links and goodwill. From small beginnings, seeds of peace grew. So much so that by 2013, UNESCO in Paris received a presentation from a Toowoomba community delegation (including the mayor, Chamber of Commerce, faith leaders and an Aboriginal artist). Those people would hardly pretend Toowoomba has everything right. We are caught up, with everyone else, in human brokenness. We know we ourselves fail and that our community often fails in our grand ideals. Yet we try to represent a sign of hope and encouragement. Indeed, the context of the UNESCO visit included Sri Lanka's continuing pain. Such situations impinge directly upon Toowoomba, where we have numerous traumatised refugees, not least from Sri Lanka, Sudan and the Congo. Our work therefore shares in the wider reconciliation the Venerable Master is actively pursuing globally, and in the continuing efforts of UNESCO and others.

Toowoomba is in many ways nowhere special. It has its gifts and charms. Australia's self-proclaimed 'Garden City', it is a hub for education, health and transport. It has a balanced economy and a sense of proportion and grace. Yet it is a regional city at the bottom of the world, distant from even the metropolitan centres clinging to the Australian coastline. Until fairly recently, it was a regional rural backwater, culturally shaped by conservative white farmer-settlers, and with a reputation as 'the buckle of the Bible belt': hardly obvious material for a 'model city'. Why then Toowoomba?, its people asked when the Venerable Master shared his dream-proposition. No obvious answer came back. Then the reality dawned. Why *not* Toowoomba? Why *not* here? Where does peace and reconciliation begin if not right now, with you and me, wherever we are?

Like life in a hall of mirrors, actual achievements in peace and reconciliation can be disproportionate. Glorious-sounding projects can amount to very little and turn quickly to dust. Yet we do ourselves a disservice when we shrink our potential. We can fail to recognise that peace and reconciliation not only starts where we are but can grow and flourish. For resurrection ripples out with every act of peace and kindness. In Toowoomba, the ripples of peace are sometimes small but also tangible. We build on a strong history of ecumenical achievement and through our faith communities we nurture Aboriginal reconciliation, refugee support, interfaith forums, friendship dinners, a Carnival Parade, and the engagement and leadership of schools, university, media and police. In the face of the wider Australian backlash against asylum seekers the city became a 'Refugee Welcome Zone' in 2013. When the city's first mosque was formally established it gave thanks to the wide community constituency which had actively enabled it. Lasting contributions have thus been laid to the community capital which is harmony's bedrock, and, through our international links, to the wider reconciliation of past and present hurts. All over the world places like Toowoomba are working on similar dreams. If not now, then when? If not here, then where? If not us, then who?

Affirmation for peace and harmony
(Toowoomba Goodwill Committee)

We come from many backgrounds and have journeyed many roads.
We give thanks for these good things of our past.
We rejoice in the first peoples of this land and their continuing cultures.
We celebrate with all who have left other nations,
brought their learning and made a home in this place.
Just as the bunya tree has given life for countless generations,
so may we offer shelter and sustenance
and share smiles of peace and harmony.

We bring many gifts and outlooks.
We give thanks for these good things of the present.
We rejoice in the strengths and diversity of our shared community.
We celebrate our many faiths and stories,
our business and our art.
Just as our environment gives delight to our Garden City,
so may we scatter seeds of understanding,
grow flowers of friendship,
plant peace and harvest harmony.

We share many hopes and dreams.
We give thanks for these promises of the future.
We rejoice in its possibilities.
We recommit ourselves to the common good.
Just as earlier diverse communities gathered
for the great Bunya festivals of the past,
so may we walk together into a more joyful and reconciling world.
Honouring our elders and raising up children of hope,
may we be a model city of peace and harmony.

Jonathan Inkpin

'TELL ABOUT IT'

'*Tena koe*, Alison' begins the e-mail, sent with a 13-hour time difference, at some implausible hour in the morning. A Māori friend is making some plans for 'entertaining' me during my extended stay in Aotearoa New Zealand. She is doing so with something of a twinkle in her eye and not a little mischief. 'I'd like to take you one weekend to the Whirinaki Forest. I'm just seeing if I can time it that my mate is home so I could maybe get some *tā moko* done and for you to meet the locals.' The land-scape of Partick, Glasgow gives way to new names and I find myself needing to reach for a dictionary to find out what it actually is she was going to get done. Never one to turn down a trip to the forest, a month or so later I find myself driving with my friend along the road from Rotorua to Murupara through thick mist and sulphur clouds, increas-ingly convinced that the tree spirits are coming alive.

It is almost midnight when we arrive at the old Principal's house of the local school, on the Marae, slip off our shoes in the porch and pad into her friend's house. Our host, a Tūhoe Māori: bushman, school teacher, hunter and extraordinary artist. The twinkle in the e-mail from my friend glittered in his eyes. 'So, what do you do?' he asks and I am, as part of the moment of welcome, called to account for the use of my time. I always know it is good for me, a Pākehā – a 'fair-skinned' person of European descent – to be in a minority. Several hundred years of exploitation, broken promises, ill kept treaties, robbery, oppression and greed crawl across my skin. There is a certain queasiness I have come to recognise amongst the Pākehā of conscience when it comes to Māori rela-tions, one which comes from the knowledge of all that has been done, and done wrong, in our name. With the Tūhoe Iwi, a particular tribe of the Māori, this is especially true, with conditions of acute oppression, violence, impoverishment and colonisation having dominated their history since the Pākehā settlers arrived. The queasiness is legitimate, as is the call to account. 'I work with refugees in Scotland,' I say, and hear the English accent for its history of empire. Here is my ancestry standing face to face with someone else's, which has fought against the Crown and Britain for rights of land, dignity, life and language. The Tūhoe Māori are also warriors. There are hunting rifles propped up in corners of the rooms and black power artwork on the walls. My account for myself feels lame and inadequate.

He laughs, and we sit at his vast kitchen table with mugs of tea. His *moko* adds animation to the mischief and twinkle in his eyes. 'We called you Pākehā "refugees",' he says. 'When you all came on those boats, they showed us pictures of the slums and houses in Glasgow you were leaving. You were refugees.' We begin a conversation which continues through my stay. It's not unlike being at Camas, the Iona Community's Centre on Mull, and indeed Camas, the deforestation of the Atlantic rainforest, and the colonisation and clearance of the Gaels and their language are my most present reference points as we share stories. He tells me of the settlement recently achieved with the government of Aotearoa New Zealand and of the process, now well underway, to restore the land to Tūhoe Māori care. He tells stories of how this was achieved. Stories of cunning and creativity, of suffering and servitude, of hope and of the need for decolonising the mind. I tell him of my time with refugees, of my time in Gaza and South Africa. These are political and human words between us. Words about land, struggle, hope and where, in each of the situations – Gaeldom, Gaza, South Africa, Aotearoa New Zealand – I come from the line, country and empire that, wittingly or not, was a perpetrator.

We walk through the bush, checking traps, tasting peppery leaves, touching the bark and creepers, looking out to Ruapehu, the active volcano on the horizon, down the gunsight of his rifle. I learn the names of trees, ridges, mountains, histories, which he shares in an English filled out with Tūhoe Māori and not a little delight in beginning here, at home, on land which has been returned.

In the workshop my friend is busy cutting out stencils of flowers for a mural. They show me the *pounamu* stones from the river. It is *taonga* – treasure – and it reminds me of walking on the north shore of Iona and stooping for pebbles – treasure too.

Sitting in the sunshine with bread and jam for breakfast – looking out over the bush, forest and mountains – he asks me if I would bring students here. 'This is a university.' There is much work to be done just in tackling the poverty, drugs and deprivation, and doing it according to Tūhoe ways; in repopulating the forest and caring for it according to Tūhoe indigenous knowledge of the bush; in the start of credit unions and factories with Tūhoe business values; in the development of a highly disciplined artistic school on the Marae: in work to live without the old enemy; and then, perhaps one day, and in their own time, make a peace with that past when something new has grown. There is nothing romantic about this work. It is a struggle, a struggle at the roots of the mind.

When it comes to the moment to leave, and drive the long winding road back through the forest, he calls us together and says an incantation over us. I recognise some words now. Not many, but the ones I hear matter. They are the words which have kept this people alive, kept this bushman hunting and gathering, kept him turning to a fusion of graffiti art and tradition to paint murals with children in his school, kept him in negotiations with the Crown to have the Treaty of Waitangi upheld, kept him speaking the language of his ancestors and close to the spirits of *hapā*, *iwi* of the *wharekai*, the gatherings of *hui* and *tangi*. I hear the place names of the Marae, the names of the places of this land: Te Urewera, Ngāputahi, Te Whāiti, Whirinaki. I hear other place names too and, though my head is bowed in prayer, I feel his eyes on me in blessing and let the words he says cover my skin like *moko*. Is this reconciliation? Is this how it happens between us as human beings. I cannot believe the privilege and honour, the unconditional hospitality of this moment. I certainly know that it is not as simple as saying words, even as a formal apology, such as those made by the Crown through the settlements. But I know that this is how perhaps we move from where we have been, to where we are not yet.

'You have travelled and seen many things and many places,' he says, after a pause and a little quiet and some movement, 'and no one knows about us here in the forest, but you know and you can tell of us.'

In her 'Instructions for living a life', the poet Mary Oliver commands us to: *'Pay attention. Be astonished. Tell about it.'*

For the queasy Pākehā of conscience, when it comes to Māori or any indigenous relations, 'telling about it' comes with the knowledge of what has been taken and done with knowledge in the name of greed. The queasiness and caution are not mistaken, are visceral, and are important ways of knowing that we have betrayed and been betrayed, that we are breakers and broken.

Yet here I am, commissioned to *'tell about it'*. And as the anthropologist Ruth Behar says: *Anthropology is nothing if it does not break your heart.*

As the road winds back though the forest, before my friend falls asleep in the sunshine after calling in at Murupara for a necessary ice lolly, we speak quietly of these things. I share my discomfort at accounting for who I am. I tell of an odd feeling that it would be easier if there were settlers and colonists in my ancestry giving grounds for an apology, or for guilt. I speak of the peculiarity of being English and nearly twenty years in Scotland. The history – both colonial and colonised – of that country in its quest for self-determination has changed and shaped me anew, and my politics – and how much more so after this encounter with the Tūhoe. I think of the sadness in my English family and friends when I say I will be voting 'Yes' in the Scottish Referendum, the sense of a new betrayal coming with what for me is a necessary part of the long, global process of decolonisation and living the apology. The queasiness of identity and politics and past remains and I wonder aloud with her, so enviably clear and proud and strong in her recovered Māori self, who my people are, and by what right – after so much betrayal – I might be of a people, and of a land.

In Andrew Greig's *At the Loch of the Green Corrie*, a book about keeping a promise to the poet Norman MacCaig, the narrator tells of his encounter with Somhairle MacGill-Eain (Sorley MacLean), who asked him: '*Who are your people?*' That question has held me. Sitting with my friend – who has just shared her answer to the question through a weekend in the Whirinaki Forest, with her people and their becoming – this question is even more acute. 'Perhaps you should write your *mihi*,' she says. 'Your way.'

Mihi

I was born in Sheffield, UK, a product of the new welfare state, to teachers. The hills I loved were Carl Wark, Higger Tor and Stanage Edge, the rivers flowed through Water-cum-Jolly Dale. In my genealogy there are no settlers that I can find, nor in my family, just farmers, butchers, weavers and the legacies of a dislocating modernity in the north of England. Grandma and Grandpa Black-burn took in strangers – the new immigrants brought from the Indian subcontinent to work the mills of Lancashire – and they took in refugees escaping from the suppression during the Prague Spring, and helped them find an occupation. Grandma and Grandpa Marham taught me to feed chickens, pigs and sheep, before feeding the village. I grew up in the cauldron of rage which was Margaret Thatcher's destruction of the hope in my city as she closed the mines, the steelworks and increased the rates of suicide in my school. I became a traveller – a Roma woman selling clothes-pegs at my door when my mother was carrying me, still unborn, said I would. My father taught me the names of the hills, flowers, trees and birds. My mother taught me to bake and to listen in hard to words. Music made me laugh and learn. Politics took root. I had never been to Soweto but it shaped the inner land-scape of my youthful soul. Languages opened me out; anthropol-ogy worked giving structure to my thoughts; theatre, liturgy and poetry gave them form.

Offenburg, St Porchaire, Durham, Biberach, Clermont, Tuebingen, Hayingen, Hornburg, Taizé, Balsall Heath.

I married Robert, and we took work in Scotland, in Glasgow – a city that was home from home. The hills became Beinn Sgritheall, Braeri-ach, Beinn A' Ghlo. I dangle my feet in the cold waters of Glenn Tilt and I swim in Martyrs' Bay on the Isle of Iona. The university became my occupation and its books and teachings made me change my life, sent me back out into the world – a vessel for grief, a 'vulnerable observer', a witness with, of words, back to learn again the lessons of hospitality of my ancestors. I choked with shame at what has been done, by the Crown, through history, in my name.

Syria, Palestine, Gaza, South Africa, Malawi, Sudan, Ethiopia, Jamaica, Jordan, Egypt, Aboriginal Australia, indigenous Canada, Aotearoa New Zealand. I read the Freedom Charter aloud from the Rivonia cell walls.

Everywhere land, stone and a meshwork of love and anger. With the years and struggles comes the love of silence and solitude. I have crossed Tongariro, climbed Mulanje, Skiddaw and Scafell Pike, worn out my shoes with walking and standing firm. I am English, Scottish, halb Schwaebin and Blen. I became poet, gardener, lover, foster mother, breadmaker, piper and a person who prays.

My friend Piki took me to Te Urewera. I listened to the forest through the bushman, on the ridge. I slept deeply, bright with stars. I think there is now a *moko* in a corner of my soul.

Tūhoe may become my new word for hope.

I am Alison ...

Alison Swinfen, Piki Diamond and Chaz Doherty, 2014

AN IONA CHRISTMAS

'Only a demanding common task builds community'

– *George MacLeod, Founder of the Iona Community*

There's a 'house party' on Iona at Christmastime. Volunteers come from all over the world to welcome guests, some of whom have been going through some very tough times all year.

I remember a gathering we had once in the Abbey common room at the end of one of those weeks, following a Communion service in the Michael Chapel.

It was like the whole world was in that room – folk from America, Poland, Wales, Pakistan …

Charles was talking to Stuart. Charles was from Hampstead Heath and Stuart was from Possilpark. Stuart had needed to get clear of where he was staying for a bit – to get away from the temptation of the drugs and drink. Stuart and Charles had seemed worlds apart. They'd barely understood each other's accents at first, and could hardly carry on a conversation around the table at mealtimes.

Joan was strumming Christmas carols on her acoustic guitar – and TJ was singing. Joan described herself as 'a radical feminist singer-songwriter/ eco-warrior priestess'; TJ played American football. He had a soft and gentle voice; subtle phrasing. There'd been some ups and downs in the week (as usual) and at one point TJ and Joan had shouted and screamed at each other in the middle of community chores. Now they were sitting making music:

'It came upon the midnight clear,
that glorious song of old,

from angels bending near the earth
to touch their harps of gold …'

In many ways it was like the end of any typical week on Iona.

Pauline and Maggie were talking to Sofija and Pristina, who were volunteers. Pauline and Maggie were sisters. Their ninety-three-year-old mother had died in September and they'd come to Iona for Christmas: because they had used to come to Iona with their father and mother when they were girls. It was a place they both loved and had felt happy: something they had in common. I glanced round the common room. Stuart and Charles were exchanging addresses now. Later, I saw the sisters sitting together in the cloisters, watching the first snowflakes fall, clouds of their breath and cigarette smoke mingling in the air.

'Thanks. I've never *had* a good Christmas,' Stuart said to me going out into the night.

'… when peace shall over all the earth
its ancient splendours fling,
and all the world give back the song
which now the angels sing …'

I went outside, in back of the Abbey; there was moonlight on the sea and I gazed up at the stars. I could see an announcement in the sky: It said that the whole world could be reconciled: brothers from Possil and Hampstead Heath, women and men, neighbours from the Balkans, estranged sisters …The world had travelled to the 'world island' of Iona to come together and be touched and healed. And the Earth is an island in the sea of the universe, I thought. A common room in God's many-roomed mansion.

And I closed my eyes and breathed in the stars and earthy night …

When I left Iona I took that announcement back. It's harder to see the stars on the mainland, with the pollution, interference, glare ... Sometimes I walk out to the country-dark to remember that night. Sometimes I need to come all the way back to Iona to be reminded of infinite possibilities.

There is no rich or poor,
no male or female:
All are one in Jesus Christ.

No black or white,
no First World or Third World:
All are one in Jesus Christ.

No 'radical feminist singer-songwriter/eco-warrior priestess',
no conservative American football player:
All are one in Jesus Christ.

No ex-junkie living in a park,
no cocaine addict wandering lost on a heath:
All are one in Jesus Christ ...

Turn off your TV screen that breeds fear
and go outside
and gaze up at the awesome sky
full of promise ...
Breathe in the stars
smell the night
Christ is born today
and every day ...

Neil Paynter

INTERNATIONAL DAY OF PEACE

21 September is the International Day of Prayer for Peace and the UN International Day of Peace ...

A prayer and words for peace

I offer you peace.
I offer you love.
I offer you friendship.
I see your beauty.
I hear your need.
I feel your feelings.
My wisdom flows from the highest Source.
I salute that Source in you.
Let us work together
for unity and peace.

Mahatma Gandhi (source unknown)

AT HOME

REFLECTIONS ON THE PRAYER OF SAINT FRANCIS

Susan Dale is a counsellor, who was involved in setting up and running a community drop-in centre in Machynlleth, Wales, following the murder of April Jones in 2013. This reflection is taken from a longer piece. (Ed.)

I am sure that I am not alone in sometimes doubting God's goodness. Sometimes, as I listen to people who have lost a loved one, or who have encountered situations that were totally outside of their control, I find myself shouting with anguish: 'God, where were you in all of this – why did you abandon this person when they needed you so much?!' Sometimes in my tears I even ask: 'God, do you exist at all? …'

Meeting with Sajela and her brother Orthie in 2010 – and listening to the story of their escape from the violence of the Democratic Republic of Congo, their journey to the UK and experiences as refugees – challenged my faith in a loving, caring God; and raised an awareness, once again, of how safe and comfortable my life is.

Sajela writes:

> *I was born in 1984 in what was then called Zaire but has now become the Democratic Republic of Congo, in a small village about twenty miles or so from Kisangani, close to the Congo River. I lived with my mother and uncle's family. I never knew my father as he had died before my birth. My memories of that place are fragmentary images: hot, muddy, potholed tracks, the forest to the edge of our village, damp and dark. The smells: sometimes of spice, sometimes of sewage; the sounds of laughter coming from children playing in an old ruined house. Singing women, brightly dressed. Once I remember going into Kisangani, walking for what seemed to me, a small child, a lifetime,*

through shack-filled hamlets towards what to all appearances was a Western-style town. Modern buildings and people selling all sorts of goods; no electricity or wages though, and little running water.

I remember hunger. Not the sort of peckish feeling that British people describe when waiting for a meal, but a day-after-day gnawing pain of not enough anywhere to alleviate that pain. This is not because the country suffers the droughts other African countries have. We have a tropical monsoon climate with high humidity and lush pastures and forest. Hunger comes, however, from war and chaos taking away our food sources. Animals killed, crops wrecked, sometimes no one to tend or sow them. Sometimes there was flooding, but not in my memory.

My family were Christian. Not the kind of hymn-singing agnostics you find in the UK, but more a kind of desperate faith mixed up with local customs and traditions.

My country, in my experience, has always been torn by war and the greed for power of man over man. Ethnic tensions: one group of people trying to show their dominance over another; I never discovered why. In 1996 there was a revolution. As a child, I did not really understand, and it is still hard to make sense of, but I think that it was when Kabila wrested power from the despot Sese Seko. The new regime was also inept, further war erupted and since then so many conflicts, each with greedy men trying to take charge by way of violence. The men, and even young boys, were taken into the armies to fight. The women chattels despoiled by capturing armies. The DRC is home to over fifty million people and is the size of Western Europe. It is not a simple conflict to understand, especially for outsiders.

There are over fifteen rebel groups and armies from many countries.

There is strand upon strand of complexity. As the Congolese saying goes: 'Power is eaten whole because power eats whole.'

Violence came to our village in 1996. It was a hot night; the rains had not come, everywhere was shimmering with heat. The black clouds sent spirals of flies onto the remaining livestock. All I remember from that night was being bundled with the other children out into the forest, into what you would probably call a hut. We were locked in and told to be quiet and still. The small children cried for their mothers. We heard the sounds of weapons, shouting, screaming; smelt the smoke of fire, but still we hid. I think we were there for three days. It was hot, airless, not easy to breathe. Our water ran out, so did the food and there were no latrines. Several small children developed a fever and two died, one of them in my arms. I was about eleven at the time. Eventually someone came for us.

What we returned to was desolation. Our village ransacked. Some of the men had been away from the village at the time; others who were there were killed. My mother and most of the women in the village had been brutally raped, some killed. It was (and still is) a political strategy that despoiling the women and planting seed in them will win the war (whatever that is about). My mother had three broken ribs, and had internal injuries which never healed. Her head had been shaved and she was pregnant with my brother. Other women had been even more brutally treated, with limbs and breasts missing. One had been beheaded and left lying in the middle of the track. These were sights no child, or adult for that matter, should have to witness. What monsters had done this? The men folk who were left alive buried the dead and rebuilt some shelters for us; this was very hard to do as so much of the landscape had been destroyed. All our livestock either perished or was taken captive. Buildings were burnt, and our water supply contaminated with some kind of oil. Trees had been hacked down. My mother never really recovered: she died in 1997 shortly after giving birth to Orthie. It was as if she gave up the will to live.

My uncle was a man of means, and well-thought-of within the community. He had been away when the ravagers had come. He and the other men decided that the girls and infants needed to flee our country of birth. He was afraid that the same fate would await us as happened to our mothers. I remember him saying that the women were the only hope for our land. Plans were made, and after my mother died they came to fruition. With the baby on my back and my cousins alongside, we started a long journey. My uncle carried all that was our life on his back. I wept as I walked, then became so tired that even weeping seemed too much effort. We took lifts occasionally, when we could, sometimes sleeping in the open, at other times finding solace from villages en route.

Eventually we walked, together with many others, into a refugee camp outside the city that is now called Kinshasa. There were miles of tent-like shacks made up of plastic and cloth, anything people could find to keep out the weather. People were dying of malnutrition, pneumonia and malaria. Two doctors from an international aid effort struggled against the overwhelming need of too many people and no provisions or facilities. Of our group of 16 from my village only my brother and I and my uncle, and one other young woman, survived. I read statistics on the Congo now and figures like 5.4 million killed since 1998 mean little unless you have witnessed the smell of death and dying, and witnessed the atrocities of raids on the villages. We were the fortunate ones. My uncle had some money, so secured us a lift to the border with

Angola. Everything within the Democratic Republic of Congo operates by way of bribes and mistrust. Everyone has an agenda, and it usually involves money changing hands, and even then often people are betrayed. We were tied into the back of jeeps under sacking, staying there for 5 days with just a few stops in the dark for water and dry bread. My baby brother sucked against my empty chest. There was nothing I could give him but single drops of water on my fingertips. Once we were stopped by militia, young boys carrying Kalashnikovs; I remember seeing them standing there, the guns nearly as tall as they were, and being so afraid. They did not speak our language; my uncle, however, still had some money and he paid them off.

Over the border in Angola we were housed and fed by some families who had come earlier. It was so good to feel a little safe. After a couple of weeks we secured a place on a small boat travelling out of Angola, headed for Spain; then we were to travel by road into France. Two days out, however, the boat got into difficulties. There were too many of us, and the sea was too rough. It lurched and drew in water, the engine failing. One passenger fell overboard and was lost. Possessions were ditched in an attempt to keep afloat. It was terrifying. There were some life jackets but not enough to go round. I managed to keep hold of my brother, but all our possessions, little though they now were, went over with everything else. Some were praying but I did not even have the courage to pray. I could not imagine a God who had let such things happen caring about us.

After a night of storm we were seen by a passing cargo vessel. They were headed, we learnt, for the UK. Big men heaved us over into first small motorised boats, then up onto the deck of a huge vessel. We learnt that we were way off course. Several days later we were picked

*up by the coast guard and taken on board their vessel, eventually being
deposited at a detention centre in the UK.*

*I still remember the feeling of so much relief at seeing this huge ship;
we hoped so much that they would see us, even though we needed to
travel unseen, but we were so desperate, and so small in the vast
ocean. They fed us bread and some kind of cereal; they also found
some milk for my brother and managed to make a feeder for him out
of a plastic water bottle and the top of a rubber glove. The relief was
overwhelming. The terror of what might happen next was as yet to
materialise ...*[1]

I once asked Sajela how all that had happened had affected her faith, and
have often reflected on her response. Working here in Machynlleth,
within a community where a young child was abducted and brutally
murdered, my faith has been challenged, but has also been a lifeline.

Sajela said: 'I try not to think of it in terms of "where was God when I
needed him", rather that he was there with me always, closer than the air
that I breathe, closer than the trauma which I see. He is the lifeblood
which has propelled me into hope.'

'Where there is doubt, faith ...'

Sometimes, Lord, I doubt my ability
to stay with the other person's pain.
The stories are so hard to tell,
and so hard to bear witness to.

Stand with me, Lord, at this time,
in this space, with this person.

Help me to find the strength
to stand alongside when all within me
is trembling and fearful.
Amen

'It is in pardoning that we are pardoned ...'

I imagine myself as someone who does not judge others and who always tries to accept people for who they are/where they are. How would I fare, though, I found myself asking, if I were to come face to face with Mark Bridger – the man convicted of murdering little April Jones. I – along with so many in the community here – have borne witness to the devastating effect of his actions on April's family, friends, neighbours, the police teams – people in their hundreds – and people across the world who have stood alongside the community.

He has admitted that he killed her, but has never spoken of where her body is. It was only small fragments of her bones that her parents finally laid to rest in a funeral service at the end of September 2013.

St Francis's sentence *'It is in pardoning that we are pardoned'* stands in stark contrast with all I feel in respect to this man. Yet he is just a man: he has children, parents, people who have loved him. He is not somehow so much set apart from all of us, who are also human.

Whilst pondering this line from the prayer of St Francis I tried to cast my mind over all the things I have done in my life which seem unpardonable, and also over any particular situations where I struggle to pardon others.

Reflecting particularly on the situation in Machynlleth, I wonder about whether forgiveness of Mark Bridger will ever be possible. Will it ever be possible to let go of the hurt and outrage? …

I talk about it with Orthie, Sajela's brother, now a young man. Orthie has recently finished college, and has gone back to the Democratic Republic of Congo as a volunteer with a small Christian organisation working with local communities in a reconciliation project with child soldiers, many of whom have been involved in violence towards the host families with whom they now live. Orthie e-mails me about his work and some of the insights he is gaining:

> *Hi Sue,*
>
> *I am well thanks. It feels really strange to be back here: the place where I was born, and yet it feels very alien and different to all my imaginings. Somehow, though, it feels like home: like the place where I belong to the earth. People look the same as me, but their experiences, their worlds are so different.*
>
> *The guys we are working with are often younger than me. Most of them have killed others; raped others. I thought this might make me feel really angry: my mother after all was the victim of just such people. I thought I would never be able to forgive. I am not sure that I do forgive, but I do know that hating eats me up, so it is better to accept and to try to make sure that these kind of things do not happen again. When one of the guys smiles at a small child in the village it feels like an outbreak of peace!*
>
> *I have been reading quite a bit, and found a poem by Pádraig Ó Tuama where he talks about the significance of the Queen shaking hands with Martin McGuinness. This says it all I think!:*

Shaking hands, by Pádraig Ó Tuama

Because what's the alternative?
Because of courage.
Because of loved ones lost.
Because no more.
Because it's a small thing; shaking hands; it happens every day.
Because I heard of one man whose hands haven't stopped shaking
since a market day in Omagh.
Because it takes a second to say hate, but it takes longer, much
longer, to be a great leader.
Much, much longer.

Because shared space without human touching doesn't amount to
much.
Because it's easier to speak to your own than to hold the hand of
someone whose side has been previously described, proscribed,
denied.
Because it is tough.
Because it is tough.
Because it is meant to be tough, and this is the stuff of memory,
the stuff of hope, the stuff of gesture, and meaning and leading.
Because it has taken so, so long.
Because it has taken land and money and languages and barrels
and barrels of blood and grieving.
Because lives have been lost.
Because lives have been taken.

Because to be bereaved is to be troubled by grief.
Because more than two troubled peoples live here.

Because I know a woman whose hand hasn't been shaken since she was a man.
Because shaking a hand is only a part of the start.
Because I know a woman whose touch calmed a man whose heart was breaking.
Because privilege is not to be taken lightly.

Because this just might be good.
Because who said that this would be easy?
Because some people love what you stand for, and for some, if *you* can, *they* can.
Because solidarity means a common hand.
Because a hand is only a hand; so hang on to it.

So join your much discussed hands.
We need this; for one small second.
So touch.
So lead.[2]

And, Sue, I have been thinking about what you said about Machynlleth where you live. I guess it will be hard for everyone to move away from being so angry with the man who murdered April, but he will not be the person who suffers from the anger – he is safely tucked up in prison! It will be the people who are feeling angry who will suffer. I know when we first spoke I was so angry with what had happened to my mum that I nearly destroyed my life. Everything and everyone around me suffered. These kids who fight … when I see them face to face I realise that they are just kids being manipulated by others, and those others are probably angry too. What good does all this anger and violence do? Letting go of it does not mean that I agree with what has happened, but it helps me to move forward and feel better about myself. I am trying to make sure that the violence stops and does not go on and on forever ...

Orthie is such a young man, but so wise. I like this idea of letting go of the anger. I wonder whether some Christian friends might see it as a 'cop-out' though. But even this letting go is so hard – when so many people here in Machynlleth have been so hurt by one person's actions; families 'ripped asunder', as one person visiting the drop-in put it. It is so difficult to let go – and I am only an outsider, a witness. I hope, however, that this letting go will enable me to find a level of peace and healing, and also an opportunity to reflect on the parts of me that I find unpardonable.

I pray that, one day, I may be able to let go enough in order to forgive, or to pardon.

'It is in pardoning that we are pardoned ...'

Lord, help me put aside my own prejudgements,
and when all those around me demand revenge,
help me to seek ways of peace and pardon.

Pardon me, Lord, at this time,
in this space, with this person.
Pardon my wrongness in the face of
all your rightness.
Amen

Susan Dale

NOTES:

1. From *The Secret Keepers: Narrative approaches to working with intergenerational trauma in families affected by childhood sexual abuse and violence*, Susan Dale, Cambridge Scholars Publishers, 2013. Used by permission of Susan Dale

2. Pádraig Ó Tuama, from *Sorry for Your Troubles*, Canterbury Press, 2012. Used by permission of Pádraig Ó Tuama

WAYS TO SEEK RECONCILIATION

The door

He said to me: *sort out your differences.*
Why should I, I thought:
it's nothing to do with me.
I have offered friendship at all times –
it was not me who avoided contact,
who didn't get in touch.

Still He said: *sort out your differences.*

Well, maybe I could make the first move,
to get in touch, to say hello;
but I am hesitant.
He pushed me a little more:
Make contact.

So I knocked on her door.

She said she wasn't feeling well,
and shut the door.
Well, Lord – I tried;
and yes, it's okay.
I will keep trying.

The room

I sit in the room –
he is opposite me,
his presence overwhelming.
The lady sits between us,
explaining the process,
putting us at our ease.

'Why are we here?' I ask,
'what has happened to us?' –
our marriage of 15 years
suddenly torn apart.

He won't tell me why.
He won't tell me what went wrong:
why his love for me died …

I say to him: 'What went wrong?'
I hear the lady say to him:
'Would you be prepared to talk
to her about this?'

He says, 'Yes.'

'A conversation over a meal, or
a meeting with a counsellor?'
she suggests.
'We will sort something out,' he says.

At last, a way of coming to terms with
what went wrong –
a way of moving forward
in friendship.

Gift of life

The aching pain, the sense of emptiness,
the desire for revenge:
my daughter murdered
by some stranger –
how do they expect me to feel?
My only daughter taken from me,
a lovely, bright girl –
her life cut short –
kidnapped and then killed.
The urge to make that man
suffer as much as I have
driving me on, keeping me going.

Then – I don't know how it happened,
why it happened.
This sense, this feeling that I was
only damaging myself in this
journey of revenge.
Realising that my life would
never be as it had been
until I got beyond
the compulsion within me.
I needed to forgive this man.

I met him ... I told him that
I had forgiven him for what
he had done to my daughter.

A huge burden was lifted from me,
my act of forgiveness
a gift of life to me
through the death of my daughter.

Katherine Rennie

THE VALUES I WOULD LIKE TO PASS ON TO MY CHILD

With regards to Palestine, peace has become a hollow word, at least to
me. People pray for peace, work for it, fund peace education
programmes, launch peace talks and initiatives, and yet peace has
remained elusive.

Growing up in Jerusalem, I always wondered why people couldn't see
the humanity in one another. But as the situation went from bad to
worse, I grew to understand why this wasn't a realistic achievement.
How do you see beyond someone's machine gun or indifference towards
you as a fellow human being as you queue at a checkpoint? How do you
see beyond someone always suspecting you? You sometimes internalise
this, and think: *Perhaps I am a threat and do not myself know it ... What do
they know about me that I don't know myself? ...*

After years of living in Scotland, I still insist to my husband that we go to the airport hours early, because I am sure I'm going to be stopped and strip-searched and the contents of my bags inspected.

Yet, there have been moments when I have seen glimmers of normal interactions where people don't behave towards each other as Occupier vs. Occupied, but as fellow human beings.

One such time was during Easter 2013, when I was visiting Jerusalem for the first time in two and a half years with my mother-in-law, Christine. On the third day of our trip, Easter Sunday, she fell and broke her leg and required surgery. It was a stressful period trying to make sure she got the best care possible, the insurance company covered her care and that we managed to get back home to Scotland safely.

One evening after leaving the hospital, my aunts, cousin and I were waiting by a bus stop within the hospital complex for my dad to bring round the car. I noticed a Jewish Orthodox woman at the stop, who kept looking over at us all the time. I thought it must be because we were talking in Arabic. Then she asked me for the time and went back to the bus stop to check the schedule, but still kept looking at us.

When my dad finally arrived, and we had all got into the car, the woman tapped on my window. I rolled it down and she directly asked my dad in Hebrew whether it would be OK for him to drive her further up the road, where she could get the tram home.

My dad said of course and she got in. She told us that she had been to visit her husband, who had a heart ailment. She and my dad chatted on about different things to do with family, and it being exhausting visiting the hospital every day; and the weather and various other mundane things. Eventually we let her off near a tram stop and she thanked my dad and we were on our way.

I marvelled at how trusting my father was: I would have been a lot more cautious. But what my dad saw was a woman who was worried about her husband and who just wanted to get home to rest, before she had to come back to the hospital again in the morning.

I have been thinking about this encounter, and many others my father has had over the years. When I used to travel with him people would always strike up conversations, like the time on the London Underground when a South African woman started chatting away with him. He would see this as the most normal thing in the world and said it was all part of the travel experience.

As I look forward to becoming a parent myself this autumn, I think of all the values that I would like to pass on to my child from my father – and especially of this ability to trust more and fear others less: to be open and to resist stereotyping people. Perhaps that is easier to practise here in peaceful Scotland, but it is still something I strive for, wherever I am.

Margo Sabella-Marshall

POVERTY AND PEACE –
REMEMBERING THE VICTIMS OF THE 'WAR ON THE POOR'

'Peace is not the silence of cemeteries …'
– Oscar Romero

An article in the *Sunday Herald* (31st May, 2015) described the current UK government welfare cuts as a *'war on the poor'*. The Scottish Council for Voluntary Organisations called it *'a humanitarian crisis'*.

Poverty is always about power. Making the most vulnerable the scapegoat for society's ills is an insidious and damaging misuse of power. The systematic removal of support from those who need it most has resulted in lives being destroyed, and this 'war on the poor' has seen many casualties. Even the government's own statistics acknowledge that many people have died as a direct result of benefit cuts.

It is important to honour and remember these individuals. A vigil was recently held at Crossbones cemetery in London. Crossbones was a graveyard for 'outcasts' where paupers and prostitutes were buried from medieval times. The names of those who have died today due to current benefit cuts were read out. Around the globe the vigil was supported by people lighting candles in sacred solidarity. People in Germany, Canada, New Zealand, America, Holland and many other places came together to form a chain of hope and care.

There are many wonderful projects in the UK seeking to support and empower those living in poverty – community-led food co-ops and gardens, campaigns and protests are enabling many to reclaim some power and make a stand. People are finding ways to peace in the 'war on the poor'. But true peace will only come through following the call to economic justice and a radical change from cruelty to compassion.

Rachel McCann

'NOTHING ABOUT US – WITHOUT US – IS FOR US': THE POVERTY TRUTH COMMISSION

Poverty is a grinding reality for millions of people in the UK today. Despite numerous government strategies and charity reports, obscene poverty continues to dominate lives.

It is our conviction that we cannot hope to understand, let alone address, the causes and symptoms of poverty unless we involve the experts. In this context, the experts are those who have a direct experience of poverty; living with the reality day in and day out. To use our motto, taken from the South African post-apartheid process: *'Nothing about us – without us – is for us.'* We believe real progress towards overcoming poverty will be made when those who experience poverty are central to the development, delivery and evaluation of solutions.

The beginning of the Poverty Truth Commission (March 2009)

The Poverty Truth Commission was formed in March 2009 after a group of people from disadvantaged communities in Glasgow testified on poverty in front of 400 people. That day, a group of Scotland's decision-makers decided to join with the testifiers, accepting that they could not address poverty without those affected.

Scotland's first Poverty Truth Commission (2009-2011)

The Commission brought together two groups of people: some of Scotland's poorest citizens and some of Scotland's most influential and strategic thinkers.

They came together out of a very special event held in Glasgow City Chambers in 2009 at which people in poverty spoke and others listened. At the end of the day, some of those who had listened (and been profoundly moved) agreed to commit themselves to an ongoing process of coming together to listen, learn and work together.

This phase of the Commission focused on three main areas of particular relevance to the Commissioners: care for children unable to live with their parents, overcoming violence in our communities, and addressing the stereotyping of people living in poverty.

In April 2011 the Poverty Truth Commission presented its findings.

The legacy stage (2011-2012)

Although the Commission planned to conclude at its formal meeting in April 2011, all members of the Commission felt they had created a special participatory model and had a very important message to spread. The

Commission spent 12 months in an important 'legacy stage' in which it sought to work with agencies committed to taking the work forward.

Second phase of the Poverty Truth Commission (2011-2014)

As a result of the connections made and interest in the Poverty Truth Commission, the original members of the Commission decided there was work still to be done – albeit with a different focus and direction. As such new commissioners were recruited and decided collectively to focus on the costs of being poor, in-work poverty, stigma, welfare cuts and food poverty.

1.Using social media to get people's stories and voices to a wider audience.

The findings of this phase of the Commission were presented at a special event: 'Turning Up the Volume on Poverty', on the 21st of June, 2014 at Glasgow's Woodside Hall: see www.faithincommunityscotland.org/wp-content/uploads/2014/06/REPORT.pdf

Now

On the 21st of June 2014 a new phase of the Commission was launched at our 'Turning Up the Volume on Poverty' event. This set of Commissioners will continue to work together until February 2016. They are focusing on food poverty, the cost of school, and dignity and people's stories.

Poverty Truth Commission/Faith in Community Scotland

Stories from the Poverty Truth Commission:
www.faithincommunityscotland.org/poverty-truth-commission/stories/
Reports and articles:
www.faithincommunityscotland.org/poverty-truth-commission/reports-and-articles/

'WE WERE A SPLENDID COMMUNITY':
ON THE REBUILDING OF IONA ABBEY

'We were a splendid community – except at mealtimes! We parsons behaved as if we were craftsmen. Attempting high-hearted happiness, we lapsed into high-handed heartiness. We knew nothing about manual work. The craftsmen were worse. Thinking they were embarked on a religious work, they tried to discard their humanity. You see, you can try to look holy for half an hour or so on a Sunday morning, but you can't look holy eight hours a day.

'Then an almighty row broke out between two of us. Someone suggested a special prayer meeting about it. When I pointed out that we already had worship in the Abbey each morning and evening, someone said, "Oh yes, that's just ordinary divine worship," implying that no one expected much to happen in ordinary divine worship.

'Thus in no time, we knew that we were the reflection of the Church which we condemned. We'd forgotten it was a carpenter who became the Eternal High Priest. And that the atonement at least means at-onement between work and worship. We had forgotten that nothing is nearer divinity than honest humanity. We'd of public worship, which is reconciliation.'

Prayer

Jesus, we ask you to make us new.
You alone are in right relations with the Father.
Only in you can we be in right relations with anyone.
Give us grace not to try to go it alone.
Give us grace to go along with you …

George MacLeod

SHARING THE PEACE

Taking children to Sunday school so they'd hear about faith from people who had some.

Staying in the crèche rather than taking the baby home again for less than an hour.

Slipping in at the back to hear the sermon because the minister seemed a good guy.

Being relieved there was a space at the back.

Realising too late it was communion – recognising the metal holders for the wee glasses.

Trying not to worry about refusing communion – I could probably just say no thanks.

Shocked that the sermon seemed personally addressed to me.

Even more shocked that the communion liturgy was too: *'You who haven't been for a long time'* …

Vague memory that 'legally' it was OK.

Received the bread and wine for the first time in a long long time.

Relieved the ceiling didn't fall in or a thunderbolt strike the window.

Someone turns and smiles, puts out their hand and says: *'Peace be with you'*.

Wow.

A hug would have been too much from a stranger but that was just right.

I was later told sharing the peace was an Episcopal or Anglican thing, but having never come across it in my life in those Churches, for me it will always be associated with the Church of Scotland.

Now I know the politics, now I know how awkward some folk find it, now I see it can sometimes be more meet-and-greet, now I see lots of things.

But I never want to forget the part it played in that service: where I just slipped in to have some child-free time because the minister seemed OK.

Now I try to be an OK minister too ...

Liz Gibson

CONSCIENCE: PEACE NOT WAR

CONSCIENCE: Peace Not War works for a world where taxes are used to nurture peace, not pay for war …

A conscientious objector is someone who, for moral or religious reasons, refuses to participate in armed conflict or to comply with conscription into the armed forces. More than 86,000 people have claimed this right since the Military Act of 1916 recognised conscientious objection to military service.

Armed conflict by states can only take place because military forces are allocated money to pay for weapons, personnel, transport, etc. States rely on our taxes so that wars can be financed and preparations for future war can be maintained. CONSCIENCE argues that every taxpayer is being conscripted into paying for military activities. Many people find this difficult or impossible to reconcile with what their inner conscience says and so have become conscientious objectors to military taxation. Some decide to withhold the part of their taxes that would go towards war and preparations for war and so become war tax resisters. This is currently illegal but is the subject of long-running legal challenges in the UK and other countries.

CONSCIENCE believes that, though we no longer face military conscription in the UK, we continue to bear a moral responsibility for war through our taxes.

CONSCIENCE campaigns for an update in the law, so that those with a conscientious objection to war can have part of their taxes spent on non-violent forms of security. Non-military security – by means of facilitating dialogues between disputing parties, greater fairness of access to essential resources, debunking of myths and false propaganda, and support for weak and fragile economies – can provide more effective long-term forms of security than military intervention.

CONSCIENCE has proposed the creation of a Peace Tax Fund: a government-managed fund to pay for non-military security to which conscientious objectors to military taxation could have the military part of their taxes allocated. Recently we discovered a little-known government organisation called the Conflict Pool, which funds conflict prevention, stabilisation and peacekeeping activities in fragile states around the world. The Conflict Pool is not yet a fund into which we can choose to direct part of our taxes but its very existence is to be encouraged and developed by those of us who are concerned to promote peace between nations. The Conflict Pool has some flaws and needs our help to develop into a more effective Peace Fund. It has been used to cover overspends on military peacekeeping operations, but recent changes have made that option less likely. There is an unhelpful lack of transparency with some of the projects funded by the Pool and two official audits have been critical of monitoring arrangements. Changes in its structure, planned for 2015, may also lead to the greater militarisation of the Pool. CONSCIENCE is campaigning towards remedying these problems and is lobbying for an increase in the amount of non-military security spending allocated via the Conflict Pool and a decreased emphasis on military peacekeeping. We are calling on government to make the management of the Conflict Pool more transparent, stop its use as an MoD slush fund, and bring a halt to creeping militarisation.

CONSCIENCE also showcases the work of non-violent peacebuilders from across the world. With our 'Meet the Real Peacebuilders' campaign we introduce to our supporters and to the wider public people who work to transform and prevent conflict across the globe. We highlight the work carried out by these individuals and organisations to show decision-makers that there are viable alternatives to securing peace through military means. It is these non-military security measures – some funded by the Conflict Pool – which we want our taxes to support.

CONSCIENCE: Peace Not War,
Archway Resource Centre,
1b Waterlow Road, London,
N19 5NJ, UK
www.conscienceonline.org.uk

Iain Farrell

A PRAYER FOR AN END TO VIOLENCE

This prayer was written on 7 July, 2005, the terrible day when four young men with bombs killed 52 people and injured 700 more in London.

— Simon Keyes

God of life,

every act of violence in our world,
between myself and another,
destroys a part of your creation.

Stir in my heart
a renewed sense of
reverence for all life.

Give me the vision to recognise your spirit
in every human being,
however they behave towards me.

Make possible the impossible
by cultivating in me
the fertile seed of healing love.

Help me play my part in breaking
the cycle of violence
by realising that
peace begins in me.

Simon Keyes
St Ethelburga's Centre for Reconciliation and Peace

THE WAR BEHIND CLOSED DOORS:
PEACE AND PERSONAL VIOLENCE

'It's like a war zone' is an often misused, misplaced phrase, casually referring to something that is chaotic or messy. Yet in terms of the impact of violence and personal trauma this phrase is appropriate. There is increasing research which recognises the damaging effect of violence on the neural pathways of the brain, and the subsequent damage to everyday life that this causes. Many people carry the emotional and physical scars of having been victims of personal violence, sometimes for the rest of their lives.

The violence that goes on behind closed doors is often a violence we struggle to discuss. Perhaps it touches on our own pain or fears? Perhaps we are embarrassed or uncomfortable with people sharing their emotions? Perhaps it is just easier if it stays hidden in the darkness?

Having worked in community and social work (including child protection), I have seen the effects of violence on individuals, families and communities. This kind of violence is often passed on from generation to generation, continuing until someone has the strength, support and opportunity to stop the cycle: until someone is able to be a peacemaker.

My own family background was violent and I have been on a powerful journey to heal, and to stop the cycle and 'be the change'. The path to peace takes hard work; it takes courage and commitment. It feels at times like walking through quicksand, but unless we are open to change, to really knowing and loving ourselves, to dwelling in peace, we will miss out on the joy, freedom and bliss of living *'life in all its fullness'* (John 10:10).

Each time we commit to transforming our own violence – which is often demonstrated in harsh comments, judging others, misplaced anger or destroying the earth's resources – we are making peace. Each time we offer safe, sacred space to someone to tell their story, free from stigma and shame, we are making peace. Each time we welcome the stranger, even when that stranger may appear 'strange', we are making peace. Each time we speak out and stand up and be counted in saying 'no more' to gender violence, to child abuse, to all acts of harm to living beings, we are making peace.

Jesus enabled many to find peace; he spent time listening deeply to others, offering healing and comfort to those whose bodies and minds had suffered violence and trauma. The distress of Legion, a man who had been chained up and who 'cut himself with stones' (Mark 5:1-20), is calmed by Jesus. Mary, the prostitute whom Jesus loved and cared for, probably experienced violence in her work. Jesus himself suffered the ultimate personal violence in his death, as those who did not understand him sought to destroy the one who embodied all that was good, all that was love, all that was radically non-violent.

Being a peacemaker in supporting others to heal, or in changing ourselves and living non-violently, is a transformative calling for all who seek to follow Christ.

Rachel McCann

ALL HUMAN BEINGS ARE VALUABLE TO GOD

I came to the Probation Service in my fifties, having been an Anglican vicar for nearly 25 years in a variety of parishes in Wales and England. I left full-time ministry due to burnout, and by a tortuous route began work, in 2008, as a Probation Officer at a hostel for some of the most dangerous, high-risk male offenders in the country, released back into the community on licence. By dangerous, I mean murderers, sex offenders and others who have committed violent crime, some of whom have made national headlines.

My hostel in Plymouth has 19 beds and our fundamental remit, indeed the fundamental principle of the Probation Service, is to protect the public and manage the risk of these offenders. An offender released on licence has to fulfil specified conditions. These conditions may include reporting to the hostel office every two hours, regular drug and alcohol testing, exclusion from a designated geographical area (usually where the victim/s reside). In addition, the people they associate with must be monitored – this is particularly important with sex offenders. The vast majority also have to attend accredited national programmes to address their offending.

Our residents are the pariahs of society and often the butt of periodic witch-hunts by the right-wing media. The two questions I'm most often asked about my work are: 'What are these people like?' and 'How can you work with such monsters?' The answers are very simple. First, if you visited the hostel and entered an informal gathering of staff and residents, you'd be hard pressed to pick out the offenders. These people with whom I share meals, play pool or darts and meet with regularly on a one-to-one basis to help them reintegrate into the community are ... human beings.

They are mostly polite and compliant and, if you take the time to dig into their past, you'll find that they have invariably been victims themselves, of sexual abuse, in the case sex offenders, or of other violence. Most suffer from some form of mental illness or personality disorder.

Often our residents feel valueless: because that is how they have been treated by society. The first thing I do with each new resident is to offer them my hand and my first name. You would be amazed at the astonishment this often engenders. However, I cannot stress enough that this is not to excuse the awful things they have done or to devalue their victim's suffering in any way. Indeed, the primary objective of the programme work residents undertake is focused on them acquiring victim empathy and an understanding of the effect that their offending has had on their victims. In some cases this is quite cathartic for them. However, for offenders who are in complete denial about their offending, this is not the case. For Probation staff, these people are the most difficult to engage with.

In short, I suppose my work can best be summed up in the old saying, which so resonates with me as a Christian: 'Hate the sin but love the sinner.'

I'll end with a parable:

Invariably I have chosen to work over the Christmas and Easter holidays, as my two sons are now grown up and I don't as yet have any grandchildren. The residents are unreservedly appreciative of those staff who come in and spend time with them on these days.

I vividly remember two Christmases ago, residents and staff sitting down together to enjoy our magnificent Christmas dinner (provided by our dedicated, ex-navy chef). As we began our meal, the bells of the parish church just down the road sounded. I glanced around the room, and I couldn't help feeling that Jesus would not have been down the road with those gathered into the fold at the church, but would be sitting down to break bread with this table of lost sheep.

I believe all human beings are valuable to God and have the possibility of redemption. When I meet with our residents, knowing the often horrendous circumstances of their upbringings, another sobering saying frequently comes to mind: 'There but for the grace of God go I.'

Neil Davies

FEEDING THE GOODNESS

Not long ago I was happy to provide a reference for a young man who was applying to serve on a police force. Having known him for eighteen years I had a fair estimate of the man. I knew him to be a person of depth, integrity, self-awareness and faith. He will be the type of officer any police force and municipality will be delighted to have.

As I worked my way through the reference form one of the questions caught my eye. It asked: *'Has the applicant ever associated with disreputable persons?'*

I knew what the question was getting at: Was the candidate a disreputable character? Was he disreputable because of the company he has kept?

Since my only options were 'yes' or 'no', I could in good conscience answer 'no'.

Had the form allowed for narrative responses, though, I may have pointed out that it would be difficult to say the same of Jesus. He intentionally and customarily dealt with disreputable people. In fact, due to his welcoming manner, they were the very people drawn to him. Desmond Tutu believes we are all designed for goodness and when we recognise that truth it makes all the difference in the world. As a result of being in close proximity to Jesus, and because he awakened the goodness in them, many of those people labelled disreputable became less so.

All of us are disreputable to one degree or another. The line between good and evil runs straight through every human heart. Our communities are not served well by police officers who think they are the 'good guys'. Indeed, our world of nations needs police officers, soldiers, civil servants, politicians and citizens wide awake to two things: *1) honesty about the good and evil present in their own souls;* and *2) a desire and commitment to look for and feed the good in themselves and others.*

Had the reference form allowed for a narrative response I may have encouraged the police department's Human Relation's people to hire the young man, but not because he refused to associate with disreputable persons. They should hire him because of his commitment to do the hard work of associating with those who are deemed disreputable, in order to identify the goodness in them and feed it.

Bill Klein

OUR WOUNDED EARTH AND EASTER HOPE

We feel it, we see it,
and for all yet unborn
we fear it.
Bewildered we wonder,
for much is unthinkable
about this shadow on the world's lung
called 'climate change'.

Can we but panic
if flood takes our homes
and crops are laid waste;
if cities lie under smog,
forests become dust
and the seasons are no more?

Maker of the seas and hills,
where are you now as the ice melts,
the willow weeps
and the songbird dies?

Light within the shining stars
and Seed of ancient oaks,
bind us again to the tears of your earth;
wake us from slumber,
to give of ourselves
in action and word;
to re-imagine a planet
not wounded, but healed.

And even in our fears,
to see anew the beauty of it all
as we encounter again
that powerful, gentle truth –
that Easter is always
a time of surprising resurrections.

Peter Millar

RECONCILIATION AS GOD'S GIFT

We face each other
across a raw divide,
the chasm of our anger
filled with the bones
of old hatreds.

The wounded earth
spews out our greed
in acrid smoke.
The gaping wound cries out in pain.

The upward surge of birds in flight;
wheeling and dancing
in the sun,
the sound of geese
strung across an empty sky,
the scent of blossom on the wind,
gifts of a generous Creator,
to lift, to call, to heal.

Kate McIlhagga

PAX VOBISCUM

Let peace fill our lives, our world, our universe.
Peace, peace, peace …
        – Universal Prayer for Peace
    used daily by members of the Iona Community

Just about everybody I know is not at peace and strives for it. So many people wake in the night disturbed by an uneasy mind, worrying about issues which, in the broad light of day, often dissolve.

For many years I have believed that it is better to live with one's worries: just accept them as a part of life. As sure as eggs is eggs, as soon as you resolve a worry or angst another one comes along to take its place. It is human nature to not be at peace. It is how we live with this, cope with it that is important.

I expect you, like me, can think of individuals, a very few, whom we have met or still know whom we see as people at peace … it quietly radiates from them. What have they got which most don't?

I had a job doing electrical work which took me into people's homes, all manner of homes: the very wealthy, the very poor. One family which stands out in my memory were living with the bare essentials of life – no carpets, no electronic gear, no ornaments – yet they oozed contented-ness. It flowed from them. They weren't simple people but they lived simple lives, appearing to crave for nothing. They were very happy with what they had and thanked God for every blessing. They made the most of every minute and everything.

Alan Hawkins

BLESS THOSE WHO WILL DIE TODAY

Bless those who will die today.
May they die in peace,
with friends at their side,
with loved ones close.
May the song of their lives
join the harmonies of heaven,
angels guide them,
Jesus greet them ...

For those who will die by violence,
for those whose death is sudden,
for those who will die amidst lights and shouts,
wires and bleeps,
may the peace of Christ be at their soul's centre,
the embrace of the Spirit surround them,
the love of the Maker
call them gently home.

Living God, bless those who will die today.
And me too, Lord, at my ending.
Amen

Chris Polhill

I WILL SEEK PEACE

PEACE BE WITH YOU

Do you mean that?
What do you mean by peace?
The absence of war?
Acceptance of the unacceptable?
The strength to cope?
The conviction that there's more to life,
that we're not alone,
that there is meaning.
Maybe it's just a phrase.
Maybe it doesn't matter what you mean by it.
Your sincerity, my sincerity …
either is a bonus but
what matters is that peace is possible.
Peace beyond understanding.
Real peace,
beginning with each and every one of us.

Liz Gibson

A PRAYER OF CONFESSION

For our incapacity to feel the sufferings of others,
and our tendency to live comfortably with injustice,
GOD FORGIVE US.

For the self-righteousness which denies guilt,
and the self-interest which strangles compassion,
GOD FORGIVE US.

For those who live their lives in careless unconcern,
who cry 'Peace, peace' when there is no peace,
WE ASK YOUR MERCY.

For our failings in community,
our lack of understanding,
WE ASK YOUR MERCY.

For our lack of forgiveness, openness, sensitivity,
GOD FORGIVE US.

For the times we were too eager to be better than others,
when we are too rushed to care,
when we are too tired to bother,
when we don't really listen,
when we are too quick to act from motives other than love,
GOD FORGIVE US.

John Harvey

GIVE US GRACE

Forgive and forget …
Let bygones be bygones …
Water under the bridge,
what's done is done,
no need to cry over spilt milk …

Easier said than done, God.
So be with us when we need to forgive.
Forgive us when we don't,
and move us to a place
where we can begin to learn your lessons of
overwhelming compassion.

Anger is a corrosive substance
and holding on to it hurts us every bit
as much as it hurts the one
we will not forgive.

When hurt holds us back …
When betrayal cuts deep …
When our sense of justice has been insulted …
When our trust has been abused …
Breathe your peace on us, O God,
and let the healing begin.

Breathe your peace on us, O God,
and give us grace …
Amen

Sally Foster-Fulton

STAND AND BE COUNTED

Creator God,
father and mother of us all,
we ask your forgiveness for our blindness:
for not understanding that violence breeds violence,
and for not doing anything about it
when we do understand.

Help us to lose our fear of testifying to the way of peace
by giving over our fear to you so that we may
'stand and be counted'.

We know in our hearts that true peace is rooted in prayer
and is received into our innermost being
by your grace,
and your grace alone.

Help us to seek the Christ-like self within us,
and to rid ourselves of self-importance and selfishness,
so that we may be as empty vessels
into which you may pour your
healing grace
so as to bring peace into our hearts,
our families, our communities,
our nations, our world.
Amen

Nia Rhosier

AN EVENING PRAYER FOR RECONCILIATION

The hardest 'word',
what comes to mind?
Sorry? Thank you? Bless you?

Reconciliation. A long hard word containing all three:
sorrow, gratitude, blessing.
A word of fault-ignoring, open-handed loving acceptance
sharing the flawed nature of all things,
silence which accepts unjudging, and judges without rejecting.

> *Gracious God of mercy,*
> *hear my prayers for reconciliation;*
> *seek out in my heart those people*
> *to whom I may be reconciled,*
> *see in me the distance I have made*
> *between myself and others.*

Prejudice. A necessary factor of having a mind,
the assumptions which make relationships possible,
the first impression which began before acquaintance,
the decision that remains after estrangement,
an undefinable taste or bias within all that is or could be.

> *Gracious God of Love,*
> *hear my prayers of contrition;*
> *sorrow for those prejudices*
> *I have allowed to jump, unbidden,*
> *to my lips, to sneak into my heart;*

the barriers I have built to keep the 'other' different,
or to steal the difference that makes others unique.

Forgiveness. A divine offering of renewal, completion,
the summation of sorrow, gratitude and blessing,
acceptance of imperfection, rejoice in the flawed
cracked, mottled world flickering in the mirror,
darkly perceived yet touched by open hearts daily.

Gracious God of Peace,
hear my prayer for those I need to forgive,
for the depth which only reconciliation can bring.
The beginning of healing
is the acknowledgement of the wound.

This evening I pray for reconciliation
in my world, on my street, in my heart.
Hear my prayers, merciful, loving, peaceful God.
Amen

Janet Foggie
Mediator at Place for Hope

MAKE US ONE

Leader: O Trinity of love,
God in community,
holy and one,
look now on us
who look to you …

ALL: AND HEAR OUR PRAYER FOR OUR COMMUNITY:

Leader: Where there is falseness …
ALL: SMOTHER IT BY YOUR TRUTH;

Leader: Where there is any coldness …
ALL: KINDLE THE FLAME OF YOUR LOVE;

Leader: Where there is joy and hope …
ALL: FREE US TO SHARE IT TOGETHER;

Leader: And make us one …
ALL: AS YOU ARE ONE.

Leader: Before God and you who are near me,
I release anything I hold against you;
I regret all I have done to harm you;
I stand beside the wrong in my life
and ask for God's forgiveness.

ALL: BEFORE GOD AND YOU WHO ARE NEAR,
WE RELEASE ANYTHING WE HOLD
AGAINST ONE ANOTHER;

WE REGRET ALL THE HARM WE HAVE DONE;
WE STAND BESIDE THE WRONG IN OUR LIVES
AND ASK FOR GOD'S FORGIVENESS.

(Silence)

Leader: Jesus says to us, each one:
'Go and sin no more,
come and follow me.'
Now bind our hands with honesty
as we offer them to each other
and our prayer to you: *(join hands if appropriate)*

Lord's Prayer …

Prayer from the Iona Community

WAITING ON THE PRINCE OF PEACE

(On John 16:33)

In the long shadows
of death-dealing,
the roiling cities
of prestige and power
where the ego-driven
are rewarded
and the humble silenced,
the little carpenter
from nowhere Nazareth,
place from whence
nothing good comes,
bids us be at peace,
satisfied with obscurity,
content to work in darkness
as we wait on dawn
and the king on a donkey.

Bonnie Thurston

FATHER GOD, CREATOR GOD

Father God, Creator God,
Holding earth and clay within your hand:
Be king to me,
Sing to me
Love within my inmost heart.

Cross of Christ crucified,
Rising o'er the ruins of our lives:
Sing to me,
Bring to me
Healing in my broken part.

Wing of God, wind of God,
Breasting high the valleys of my heart:
Bring to me,
Wing to me
Peace within my inmost heart.

Wing to me,
Sing to me
Peace within my inmost heart.

Lizzie Ballagher

(This prayer was set to music and recorded by the pianist Keith Routledge, on the album Inspirational Piano, *Authentic Music, 2008.)*

A LITANY ON THE PRAYER OF SAINT FRANCIS OF ASSISI

Lord, make us instruments of your peace,

> Lead us to embrace the war-torn world;
> lead us to present our bodies on the violent streets –
> to cry out for justice and plant the seeds of peace.

where there is hatred, let us sow love;

> Hatred spews from radios and the mouths of so-called leaders.
> They say that Love is weakness.
> Give us the courage of Jesus to sow strong Love.

where there is injury, pardon;

> So many of us have been injured by poverty, prison, violence,
> hunger and homelessness.
> Help us to welcome the justice of the Beloved Community
> where forgiveness will bring new life.

where there is doubt, faith;

> Modern life whizzes by in a cacophony of noise and images.
> Help us to be still and quiet,
> to know you are the Holy One,
> and to see you in the face of the poor.

where there is despair, hope;

> Our land is awash in the tsunami of despair, O God!
> Please reach out your hand

and make a way out of no way.

where there is darkness, light;

> The people who walked in darkness have seen a great light:
> those who dwell in the land of the shadow of death,
> on them the light has shined. (Isaiah 9:2)

and where there is sadness, joy.

> Oppression dehumanises us all:
> oppressed and oppressor alike.
> Show us the path to justice that we might break the chains
> and embrace the freedom that brings joy and abundance for all.

O Divine Leader,

> You are the Holy One.
> Only you can show us how to throw off
> the system of domination and empire.
> Yours is the Beloved Community.

grant that we may not so much seek
to be consoled, as to console;

> Blessed are those who mourn,
> for they shall be comforted. (Matthew 5:4)

to be understood, as to understand;

> Give us ears to hear
> and hearts to understand.

to be loved as to love;

> And now faith, hope and love abide,
> these three;
> and the greatest of these is love.

for it is in giving that we receive;

> Ask, and it will be given you;
> seek, and you will find;
> knock, and the door will be opened for you. (Matthew 7:7)

it is in pardoning that we are pardoned;

> Forgive us our wrongs,
> as we forgive those who have wronged us.

and it is in dying that we are born to eternal life.

> We know love by this,
> that Jesus laid down his life for us –
> and we ought to lay down our lives
> for one another. (1 John 3:16)

Murphy Davis
Open Door Community, Atlanta, Georgia

GOD OF WORDS MADE FLESH

Glorious God,
so often our lives are lived in hesitancy:
cautious in our love,
careful in our generosity.
Your life was one of upturned tables,
perfumed feet and extravagant meals.

So often we live lives of incessant busyness,
of guilt-ridden failure to meet
all the demands and expectations.
You embraced the untouchable
and then withdrew in silence,
sustained by love and solitude,
by sleep in the middle of the storm.

God, form your ways in us
that our lives would bear the hallmark of your love.
We remember the needs of others –
the desperation of those crying out for a meal,
pleading for freedom from pain,
fearful of the hatred that surrounds them.

Who are we in the face of such suffering?
What can we offer against the torrent of injustice?
Forgiveness, compassion, generosity:
fragile aspiration in such lofty words.

God of words made flesh,
let your Holy Spirit overshadow our lives
and the lives of your people around the world,
that forgiveness, compassion and generosity
would take on human flesh,
walk the earth
and transform the world.

David McNeish

I WILL SEEK PEACE

I will seek peace at heart
Try to overcome my fears, my anxieties and troubled,
anxious mind
I will look for solace
Search for comfort
I will seek peace at heart

I will seek peace at home
Reach out to those
who are victims of abuse
through age or gender or sexuality
I will challenge those who are perpetrators
Speak up for those who have no voice
I will seek peace at home

I will seek peace in the virtual world
Encourage young and old to dream the right dreams,
live creatively,
have real adventures –
which are free from violence or aggression
I will seek peace in the virtual world

I will seek peace with the earth
I'll campaign for the forests
Buy fairtrade products, recycle, keep a compost
and wonder at the beauty of nature
I will seek peace with the earth

I will seek peace in the marketplace
Live humbly and responsibly
Share my wealth and my home
Stand up for the rights of the poor and exploited
I will seek peace in the marketplace

I will seek peace not war
Study non-violence, resolve conflict,
campaign against arms, lobby governments
and challenge apathy
I will seek peace not war

And in my seeking I will live with hope
Strive for change
Act with humility … courage … and faith
And choose love not hate.

Neil Squires

Written for worship at an Iona Community plenary

SOURCES AND ACKNOWLEDGEMENTS

Several pieces in this book were first published in *Coracle*, the magazine of the Iona Community, Neil Paynter (Ed.): www.iona.org.uk

'On meek refusal', from *Seeking Justice: the Radical Compassion of Jesus*, Keith Hebden, Christian Alternative, www.christian-alternative.com, forum@jhp-books.net. Used by permission of Keith Hebden and Christian Alternative

'George' – by Neil Paynter, from *Down to Earth: Stories and Sketches*, Neil Paynter, Illustrations by Iain Campbell, Wild Goose Publications, 2009

'Easter address at Faslane submarine base, April 12, 2014', by Alastair McIntosh, first published in *The Friend*. Used by permission of Alastair McIntosh

'A peaceful land' – by Kathy Galloway © Kathy Galloway

'The Archbishop chairs the first session' – by Ingrid de Kok, from *Seasonal Fires: New and Selected Poems*, by Ingrid de Kok, published by Umuzi in South Africa and Seven Stories Press in the USA, 2006. Used by permission of Ingrid de Kok © Ingrid de Kok

'The land of unlikeness: churches and reconciliation', by David Stevens, from the *Land of Unlikeness: Explorations into Reconciliation*, Columba Press, 2004. Used by permission of the Corrymeela Community and Columba Press

'Praying with the earth' – by John Philip Newell © John Philip Newell

'The Nonviolent Peaceforce meet the arrow boys' – by Mel Duncan © Mel Duncan, Nonviolent Peaceforce

'The small girl and the big men: Nonviolent Peaceforce – by Mel Duncan © Mel Duncan, Nonviolent Peaceforce

'An Iona Christmas', by Neil Paynter, from *Good News of Great Joy: Daily Readings for Advent from Around the World*, by Peter Millar and Neil Paynter, Wild Goose Publications, 2010

'Nothing about us – without us – is for us' – from the Poverty Truth Commission website: www.faithincommunityscotland.org/poverty-truth-commission. Used by permission of the Poverty Truth Commission

'We were a splendid community ...', George MacLeod, from the BBC film *Can These Bones Live?*, 1964, quoted in *George MacLeod: A Biography*, Ron Ferguson, Wild Goose Publications, reprinted 2004

'Jesus, we ask you to make us new ...', by George MacLeod, from the prayer 'Where freedom is, and laughter', from *The Whole Earth Shall Cry Glory: Iona Prayers*, George MacLeod, Wild Goose Publications, 1985, 2007

'CONSCIENCE: Peace Not War' – by Iain Farrell © Iain Farrell, CONSCIENCE: Peace Not War

'Reconciliation as God's gift' – by Kate McIlhagga, from *The Green Heart of the Snowdrop*, Kate McIlhagga, 2004, Wild Goose Publications ©

'A prayer of confession', by John Harvey, from the download 'Swords into Ploughshares: A simple liturgy on peace and non-violence', John Harvey, Wild Goose Publications

'Stand and be counted', by Nia Rhosier, was first published in *Timeless Prayers for Peace*, Geoffrey Duncan, Canterbury Press, 2003. Used by permission of Nia Rhosier

'Make us one' – from *Iona Abbey Worship Book,* Wild Goose Publications, 2001 © Iona Community

'A litany on the Prayer of Saint Francis of Assisi – by Murphy Davis © Murphy Davis, Open Door Community

SOME WEBSITES

Alastair McIntosh: *www.alastairmcintosh.com*

Conscience: Peace Not War: *www.conscienceonline.org.uk*

Ecumenical Accompaniment Programme in Palestine and Israel: *www.eappi.org/en*

Fellowship of Reconciliation: *http://for-scotland.org.uk/*

Glasgow Refugee, Asylum and Migration Network: *http://gramnet.wordpress.com*

International Day of Peace: *http://www.un.org/en/events/peaceday/*

International Day of Prayer for Peace: *www.oikoumene.org/en/press-centre/events/international-day-of-prayer-for-peace*

John Philip Newell/Heartbeat: *http://heartbeatjourney.org/*

Keith Hebden/Compassionistas.net: *http://compassionistas.net/wordpress/author/keith-hebden/*

Nonviolent Peaceforce: *www.nonviolentpeaceforce.org*

Place for Hope: *www.placeforhope.org.uk*

Pure Land Learning College: *www.purelandcollege.org.au*

St Ethelburga's Centre for Reconciliation and Peace: *www.stethelburgas.org*

The Corrymeela Community: *www.corrymeela.org*

The Iona Community: *www.iona.org.uk*

The Open Door Community: *http://opendoorcommunity.org/*

Theme-centred Interaction (TCI): *www.ruth-cohn-institute.org/home.html*

THE RULE OF THE IONA COMMUNITY

As Members of the Iona Community we commit ourselves to:

1. Daily prayer, worship with others and regular engagement with the Bible and other material which nourishes us

2. Working for justice and peace, wholeness and reconciliation in our localities, society and the whole creation

3. Supporting one another in prayer and by meeting, communicating, and accounting with one another for the use of our gifts, money and time, our use of the earth's resources and our keeping of all aspects of the Rule.

4. Sharing in the corporate life and organisation of the Community.

Associate members are invited to keep the Rule whereas full members are held accountable for their keeping of the Rule.

Justice, Peace and Integrity of Creation Commitment

We believe:

1. that the Gospel commands us to seek peace founded on justice and that costly reconciliation is at the heart of the Gospel;

2. that work for justice, peace and an equitable society is a matter of extreme urgency;

3. that God has given us partnership as stewards of creation and that we have a responsibility to live in a right relationship with the whole of God's creation;

4. that, handled with integrity, creation can provide for the needs of all, but not for the greed which leads to injustice and inequality, and endangers life on earth;

5. that everyone should have the quality and dignity of a full life that requires adequate physical, social and political opportunity, without the oppression of poverty, injustice and fear;

6. that social and political action leading to justice for all people and encouraged by prayer and discussion is a vital work of the Church at all levels;

7. that the use or threatened use of nuclear and other weapons of mass destruction is theologically and morally indefensible and that opposition to their existence is an imperative of the Christian faith.

As Members and Family Groups we will:

8. engage in forms of political witness and action, prayerfully and thoughtfully, to promote just and peaceful social, political and economic structures;

9. work for a policy of renunciation by our own nations of all weapons of mass destruction and for the encouragement of other nations, individually or collectively, to do the same;

10. celebrate human diversity and actively work to combat discrimination on grounds of age, colour, disability, mental wellbeing, differing ability, gender, race, ethnic and cultural background, sexual orientation or religion;

11. work for the establishment of the United Nations Organisation as the principal organ of international reconciliation and security, in place of military alliances;

12. support and promote research and education into nonviolent ways of achieving justice, peace and a sustainable global society;

13. work for reconciliation within and among nations by international sharing and exchange of experience and people, with particular concern for politically and economically oppressed nations.

14. act in solidarity with the victims of environmental injustice throughout the world, and support political and structural change in our own countries to reduce our over-consumption of resources.

ABOUT THE CONTRIBUTORS

Tim Aldred is Head of Policy and Public Affairs at the Fairtrade Foundation.

Lizzie Ballagher is Poet in Residence of the South Downs Way.

Susan Dale works as a psychotherapist and narrative researcher and writer. She is a member of the Iona Community.

Neil Davies: I was born in Cardiff and grew up in Llantrisant, a village at the mouth of the Welsh mining valleys. My family were valley folk who worked in the mines. Being Vicar of Aberfan during the 1983/84 miners' strike and a four-month visit to South Africa in 1977 were formative experiences in fuelling my concern about injustice in the world. Since writing this piece I have moved on to delivering programmes on domestic violence and thinking skills to offenders. I have been a member of the Iona Community since 2007.

Murphy Davis is a co-founder, with her husband, Eduard Loring, of the Open Door Community in Atlanta, Georgia. Open Door is a residential community in the Catholic Worker movement, which seeks to dismantle racism, sexism, heterosexism and violence, abolish the death penalty and war and proclaim the Beloved Community through loving relationships with some of the most neglected and outcast of God's children: the homeless and our sisters and brothers in prison.

Open Door members serve meals, provide showers and clean clothes, staff free medical and foot clinics, worship and share Eucharist together, and meet for the clarification of thought. They have a prison ministry, including monthly trips for families to visit loved ones in various prisons in Georgia, and they advocate on behalf of the oppressed, homeless and prisoners through non-violent protests, grassroots organising and the publication of their monthly newspaper, *Hospitality*. The Open Door Community welcomes short and long-term volunteers to join the work. Open Door is one of the Iona Community's sister communities.

Ingrid de Kok has written five books of poetry, most recently *Other Signs* (Kwela Books, 2011). Her work has been widely anthologised and has been translated into nine languages. It is taught in South Africa and around the world. She has read at major national and international festivals and has been awarded residencies and fellowships abroad, and national awards. She lives in Cape Town. Her website is: http://ingriddekok.co.za/

Piki Diamond and Chaz Doherty: 'authors of hospitality and Māori artists, teachers and learners'.

Mel Duncan is co-founder of Nonviolent Peaceforce and a former Iona Community volunteer.

Dagmar Erdmann was part of the Iona Community's Resident Group on Iona, and is now a midwife in Germany.

Dr Iain Farrell has been a supporter of CONSCIENCE since it began in the 1980s as The Peace Tax Campaign. His professional background is in science teaching and management in the independent education sector.

Rev Dr Janet Foggie is a mediator with Place for Hope. Her prayer was originally written for an evening of worship, in Dundee, reflecting on the troubles in Northern Ireland. Place for Hope, rooted in Scotland and working across all boundaries, accompanies and equips people and faith communities so that we are more able to be peacemakers and to navigate conflict well. The vision of Place for Hope is *'for a world where people embrace the transformational potential of conflict and nurture the art of peacebuilding'*.

Sally Foster-Fulton is Convener of the Church and Society Council of the Church of Scotland and is an occasional guest on BBC radio and television.

Kathy Galloway is Head of Christian Aid Scotland and a former Leader of the Iona Community.

Liz Gibson worked backstage in theatre and sold books, before training for ministry in the Church of Scotland. After moving from Edinburgh to Oban with her husband and two sons, she spent five years as Associate Minister and Hospital Chaplain, followed by five years living in Dalmally as Parish Minister for Glenorchy & Innishael linked with Strathfillan. She then decided to 'do ministry differently' and moved to a croft on the Isle of Mull in 2013. She and Martyn welcome short-term guests in return for donations and/or helping on the croft. Through WWOOF UK people from a range of countries have spent time clearing bracken, planting fruit and tea and in many other permaculture-based activities. Liz continues to preach and offer pastoral care on a supply and locum basis, spending several weeks a year on the neighbouring island of Colonsay. Arts and crafts increasingly feature in her work. She has been a member of the Iona Community since 1998.

Rick Goodwin is the Clinical Services Manager of the Men's Project in Ottawa, Canada. Rick's experience includes lecturing at both the college and university level, and training helping professionals on issues of male sexual trauma, gender, and ending violence. He has a clinical practice as well, focusing on group trauma treatment for men. Training in gender and violence has taken him to Jamaica, England, the United States, Cambodia as well as India, where he conducted gender sensitivity training to male directors of social service agencies. He can be reached at rgoodwin@1in6.ca

John Harvey was a member, with his wife, Molly, of the Gorbals Group Ministry in the 1960s, and a parish minister in Gorbals, Govan, and Raploch in Stirling. He was Warden of Iona Abbey for five years in the 1970s, and Leader of the Iona Community from 1988 to 1995. He has been a member of the Iona Community since 1964.

Molly Harvey is a member of the Iona Community.

Ruth Harvey is Head of Training and Peacebuilding at Place for Hope. She is a member of the Iona Community, living in Cumbria, and is the author of a number of publications, including 'Live in the Light: Reflections on peacemaking and reconciliation' (Wild Goose Publications).

Alan Hawkins is an associate member of the Iona Community living in Kilmartin, Argyll. He is a volunteer driver with the Mid Argyll Transport Volunteers and is passionate about the environment and all that is in it.

Keith Hebden is a parish priest and Seeking Justice deanery advisor in Mansfield, Nottinghamshire, where he chairs the Diocesan Greener Churches Group. He teaches and writes on practical theology and spirituality.

Jonathan Inkpin is an Anglican priest who has held a range of local, regional and national ministerial positions in his native England and in Australia. He is a member of the Wellspring Community in Australia and is currently Rector of St Luke Toowoomba.

Simon Keyes is a former Director of St Ethelburga's Centre for Reconciliation and Peace. St Ethelburga's Centre for Reconciliation and Peace was created from the ruins of the mediaeval church destroyed by the IRA's Bishopsgate bomb in April 1993. Since it reopened in 2003, more than 100,000 people from all round the world have met there to share stories, ideas and skills to help build relationships across divisions of conflict, culture and religion.

Bill Klein: An associate member of the Iona Community since 1977. Currently a Presbyterian Church (USA) pastor of the Lexington Presbyterian Church, Lexington, VA. Married to Deb, associate member as well.

George MacLeod was the founder of the Iona Community.

Rachel McCann is a gardener, activist and former social worker, who lived and worked alongside people in poverty for many years.

Kate McIlhagga was a minister and a member of the Iona Community until her death in 2002.

Alastair McIntosh: Raised on the Isle of Lewis and resident in Govan, Alastair is a Quaker and the author of several books, including *Soil and Soul* (Aurum Press); *Hell and High Water* (Birlinn) and *Island Spirituality* (The Islands Book Trust). He is a founding director of the GalGael Trust and a Fellow and special advisor to the Centre for Human Ecology (CHE).

David McNeish is a minister and singer/songwriter working and living in the west mainland of Orkney with Sally (a primary teacher) and their three children. Prior to ministry, David worked as a campaigner for the CAB service, a worship musician and a hospital doctor, though not all at the same time. He is a member of the Iona Community.

Elisabeth Christa Miescher is a graduate teacher of Theme-centred Interaction (TCI), a former Ecumenical Accompanier and a member of the Iona Community in Switzerland.

Peter Millar is a member of the Iona Community, a soul friend to many and an activist and writer.

Yvonne Morland is a member of the Iona Community.

The Revd Dr *John Philip Newell* is a poet, peacemaker and scholar. Formerly Warden of Iona Abbey, he is now Companion Theologian for the American Spirituality Center of Casa del Sol at Ghost Ranch in the high desert of New Mexico where he and his wife spend their summers. John Philip is the co-founder of Heartbeat: A Journey Towards Earth's Wellbeing, and is the author of over 15 books, including *Listening for the Heartbeat of God* (Paulist Press), *Praying with the Earth* (Eerdmans/SCM-Canterbury Press) and *A New Harmony: the Spirit, the Earth, & the Human Soul* (Jossey-Bass).

Paul Nicolson works with Taxpayers Against Poverty and is an associate of the Iona Community.

Lesley Orr is a historian and a member of the Iona Community.

Bryan Owen, a retired teacher and minister, was an International Election Observer for the European Union in the Balkans. All of the elections were in post-conflict situations and the poem in this book grew out of what he witnessed and was told about in Kosovo, Serbia and Albania. Aung San Suu Kyi's observation seemed to make sense. If there were no men resurrecting old enmities rooted way back in history, the world would be a very different place.

Catherine Oxworth is a child of God who hopes to leave the world a better place through the gift of her life. She is at heart a curious musician and artist, with a passion for learning, and sharing that passion with others. Catherine is currently completing a PhD in education in order to give voice to young girls in Kenya and Zambia. Catherine would like her epitaph to read, 'She tried!'

Neil Paynter is an editor, writer and late-night piano player, who lives with his partner Helen, his mum and Stevie the cat in a flat in Biggar. He is the author of *Down to Earth: Stories and Sketches* (Wild Goose Publications).

Chris Polhill is a member of the Iona Community and one of the first women priests in the Church of England. She has contributed to a number of Wild Goose books and is the author of *Eggs and Ashes* (with Ruth Burgess), *A Pilgrim's Guide to Iona Abbey*, *A Heart for Creation* and *In the Mists on the Shoreline*. She and her husband John run the Reflection Gardens, which highlights the Christian spiritual journey and environmental issues.

Rosemary Power is an Iona Community member who lived in the north of Ireland, including in Belfast from 1986-92, during the time of the Troubles.

Benjamin Pratt is a United Methodist minister who worked for many years as a pastoral counsellor. He is an author and an advocate for caregivers. His books include *A Guide for Caregivers* and *Short Stuff from the Tall Guy: Lenten Meditations on Seeking Peace in a Troubled World*. Benjamin lives near Washington D.C. with his wife, Judith.

John Rackley is a Baptist minister who lives in Leicestershire.

Katherine Rennie is a trained mediator, a Local Preacher with the Methodist Church and a member of the Iona Community.

Nia Rhosier is the Custodian of the Centre for Christian Unity, Renewal & Peace at Pontrobert, Montgomeryshire.

Margo Sabella-Marshall has worked in humanitarian aid and development in Palestine, and in policy with the Scottish Government. She is now mother to a beautiful baby girl.

Neil Squires is an associate of the Iona Community.

Helen Steven is a peace activist, Quaker and a member of the Iona Community. She is the author of *Roger: An Extraordinary Peace Campaigner* (Wild Goose) and *No Extraordinary Power: Prayer, Stillness and Activism* (Quaker Books).

David Stevens is a former Leader of the Corrymeela Community. David died on 23rd May, 2010.

Jan Sutch Pickard has twice served as a peace monitor with the Ecumenical Accompaniment Programme in Palestine and Israel. As part of a small international team, she was based in the West Bank village of Yanoun in 2010. Since then, the illegal Israeli settlements have expanded and the villagers have lost much more of their land and olive trees … Jan is a former Warden of Iona Abbey, a writer and storyteller and a Methodist lay preacher.

Alison Swinfen is Co-Convener of Glasgow Refugee, Asylum and Migration Network and is a member of the Iona Community.

Bonnie Thurston: After years as a university professor, Bonnie Thurston lives quietly in her home state of West Virginia, grows things and volunteers at a local soup kitchen and a food pantry. She has authored or edited many theological books, most recently *Maverick Mark: The Untamed First Gospel* (Liturgical Press) and *O Taste and See* (Paraclete Press). Her most recent collections of poetry are *Practising Silence* (Paraclete Press) and *A Place to Pay Attention* (Cinnamon Press).

Margery Toller is a member of the Iona Community.

Reinhild Traitler-Espiritu has worked with the World Council of Churches in Geneva and was Director of the Protestant Academy Boldern, near Zurich. For the past 20 years she has been involved in interreligious dialogue at various levels. She is the co-editor of *Towards a Pedagogy of Interreligious Diversity* (EPIL), and is a member of the Iona Community.

Iain Whyte is a former anti-Apartheid activist, author of *Scotland and the Abolition of Black Slavery* (Edinburgh University Press) and a member of the Iona Community.

WILD GOOSE PUBLICATIONS IS PART OF THE IONA COMMUNITY

- An ecumenical movement of men and women from different walks of life and different traditions in the Christian church
- Committed to the gospel of Jesus Christ, and to following where that leads, even into the unknown
- Engaged together, and with people of goodwill across the world, in acting, reflecting and praying for justice, peace and the integrity of creation
- Convinced that the inclusive community we seek must be embodied in the community we practise

Together with our staff, we are responsible for:

- Our islands residential centres of Iona Abbey, the MacLeod Centre on Iona, and Camas Adventure Centre on the Ross of Mull

and in Glasgow:

- The administration of the Community
- Our work with young people
- Our publishing house, Wild Goose Publications
- Our association in the revitalising of worship with the Wild Goose Resource Group

The Iona Community was founded in Glasgow in 1938 by George MacLeod, minister, visionary and prophetic witness for peace, in the context of the poverty and despair of the Depression. Its original task of rebuilding the monastic ruins of Iona Abbey became a sign of hopeful rebuilding of community in Scotland and beyond. Today, we are about 250 Members, mostly in Britain, and 1500 Associate Members, with 1400 Friends worldwide. Together and apart, 'we follow the light we have, and pray for more light'.

For information on the Iona Community contact:
The Iona Community, Fourth Floor, Savoy House, 140 Sauchiehall Street,
Glasgow G2 3DH, UK. Phone: 0141 332 6343
e-mail: admin@iona.org.uk; web: www.iona.org.uk

For enquiries about visiting Iona, please contact:
Iona Abbey, Isle of Iona, Argyll PA76 6SN, UK. Phone: 01681 700404
e-mail: ionacomm@iona.org.uk

Wild Goose Publications, the publishing house of the Iona Community established in the Celtic Christian tradition of Saint Columba, produces books, e-books, CDs and digital downloads on:

- holistic spirituality
- social justice
- political and peace issues
- healing
- innovative approaches to worship
- song in worship, including the work of the Wild Goose Resource Group
- material for meditation and reflection

For more information:

Wild Goose Publications
Fourth Floor, Savoy House
140 Sauchiehall Street,
Glasgow G2 3DH, UK

Tel. +44 (0)141 332 6292
Fax +44 (0)141 332 1090
e-mail: admin@ionabooks.com

or visit our website at
www.ionabooks.com
for details of all our products and online sales